Cook, Cat and Colander

Ann Hill Workman

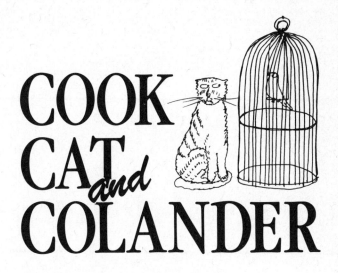

COOK
CAT *and*
COLANDER

Illustrated by Jill Cox

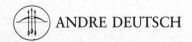 ANDRE DEUTSCH

First published 1985 by André Deutsch Limited
105 Great Russell Street London WC1

An edited extract of 'Full of Eastern Promise' has
appeared in *Good Housekeeping*. An earlier version of
'Sweet Revenge' has appeared in *Honey*.

British Library Cataloguing in Publication Data

Workman, Ann Hill
  Cook, Cat and Colander
  1. Domestics—England
  I. Title
  640'.46'0924   HD8039.D52G7
ISBN 0-233-97742-2 - 5

Phototypeset by Wyvern Typesetting Limited, Bristol
Printed in Great Britain by Ebenezer Baylis & Son, Worcester

To Ian, with love, for the confidence

Contents

Prologue

Anyone observing me sitting on the bottom tread of the stairs, clad in pink shortie nightie and red frilly apron, clutching a telephone in one hand and a resentful Cat in the other whilst simultaneously keeping my eyes glued to the letterbox, could have been forgiven for assuming that here was a woman under the influence. And they would have been quite right; but it was the influence of strong emotion I was under, not strong drink. I was waiting, on tenterhooks, for My Life to Change.

Deciding on this completely new way of life was a bit like deciding to go for a swim on Christmas Day; it was no good just dipping a toe in here, a finger there. It had to be accomplished swiftly, bravely and decisively: the only method was to take a deep breath, leap in at the deep end and damn the consequences. A horrible shock to the system at first, but, with any luck, invigorating once one was in. I had long nurtured the notion of becoming a cook-housekeeper, should I ever find myself homeless or alone in the world; perhaps some time in the far distant future, when I was in my late fifties or early sixties – a stage of life which seemed, at the time, immeasurably remote. And now, in one drastic year, circumstances had made it necessary for this contingency plan to be put into operation if I was to continue my ingrained, lifelong habit of having a roof over my head and one square meal a day.

I had no idea of how to set about implementing the plan. I knew no one in the business, had no experience apart from that of running the usual family home, and no idea about wages or conditions. Obviously the first step was to peruse the columns of those papers and periodicals in which people in a position to hire domestic help advertised.

9

I rushed down to the local paper shop and invested in the *Lady* and the *Telegraph* – the newsagent was intrigued by these respectable purchases in lieu of my usual *Private Eye* and *Mad Magazine* – plus some stationery and stamps. Letters of such importance needed to be typed on the best cream-laid – or would it be more suitable to use blue-lined, with painstaking handwriting? In the end I compromised and settled for the good paper and my usual arthritic-spider scrawl. I was quite overwhelmed by the pages and pages of Dom. Sits. (Vac.) and in my innocence even contemplated applying for those which offered accommodation only, in return for help with house, garden or children. (Fortunately my mercenary streak came to the rescue before I could do anything so foolish.) The columns provided fascinating reading and I went over them until I knew them practically by heart, marking those that looked promising with a red tick and those even remotely possible with a blue one. It was fun.

My choice was, however, more restricted than it might have been, because I needed a job where Cat would be acceptable. Not welcome; that was too much to ask for. If Cat couldn't go, neither could I; apart from the fact that she had owned me for years and I loved her dearly, I couldn't possibly farm her out to friends. If I wanted them to remain friends, that is. Cat appealed to very few people, being a one-woman feline given to attacking all and sundry totally without prejudice, including me – and I was the one most often in the firing line. It was a case of swings and roundabouts. She was destructive, bullying and rarely affectionate, and I wouldn't have swapped her for the Crown Jewels; whither I went, there wenteth Cat, and that ruled out a lot of advertisers who stipulated 'no pets'.

Finally, with fingers crossed, I wrote off to several unsuspecting people in the non-pet-banning category, and waited nervously for their replies. The die was cast; I was determined to become a cook-housekeeper. Goodbye typewriter, adieu shorthand, farewell the nine-to-five desk to which I was so accustomed. I wasn't just changing my job, I was changing my whole way of life. That is, if anyone replied. Just to fool the fates into ensuring that someone did, I went out and bought a stack of remnants and made myself seven assorted frilly aprons, all of which subsequently turned out to be quite unsuitable.

After that, I sat on the stairs within easy reach of both phone and letterbox, and waited. Cat waited with me. We'd been through a lot together, Cat and I. It was as nothing compared to what lay in store for us now.

Crumbling Court

'I'll expect you at four, then. I do hope we'll be able to come to some arrangement – I do so need someone nice to look after me.' The phone went dead and, all unbeknownst to me, my fate for the next eighteen months was sealed. The caller on the phone was one of the five to whose advertisements I had hopefully replied; brave people indeed, because I'd been very honest about my lack of experience. Or perhaps they were just desperate; good help is hard to come by, as I was going to learn, along with all the other new skills and unsuspected arts of the professional cook-housekeeper. Such as how to cope with a sudden influx of guests, how to con your employer that yes, the polishing has been done, and how to make small economies and profits – all strictly above-board, of course . . .

With heart in mouth, I set off for the interview, giving myself plenty of time to find the place – a remote country house. Just as well I allowed that extra hour, because I drove past the entrance twice before realising that the rusty gate hanging askew from its post was the place to aim for. It hardly seemed to fit the elegance inferred by the letterhead. Neither did the dank driveway, overhung with gloomy, dripping trees and plentifully potholed; the car bounced and juddered up half a mile of what looked like No-Man's-Land before coming to a grateful halt in front of what can only be described as an ancestral pile. 'Heap' might have been even more appropriate. The place hadn't seen a lick of paint in years; window shutters, like the entrance gate, hung crookedly; weeds and ferns flourished on the roof and in cracks between the bricks. Over the front door a length of guttering hung down like the sword of Damocles. The whole place was straight out of the Munsters, and I fully expected as I pulled the front-door bell (yes! a bell-pull) that the faint far-off clang would be answered by the arrival of a funereal butler with something distinctly odd about the neck.

I needn't have worried. Footsteps padded to the door, which opened to reveal an extremely small, very old and extraordinarily-dressed lady. She wore what appeared to be a selection of jumble-sale rejects, topped by a sacking apron and a man's very long cardigan; diamond earrings swung from her wrinkled earlobes, her white hair was pinned in a wild bird's nest on top of her head, and the whole startling ensemble was set off nicely by ancient wellies. It was my first, and typical, sight of Little Madam who, although I didn't realise it at the time, was to give me the gentlest, kindest, most eccentric introduction to my new station in life.

'Come in, my dear, I've just been down in the cellar,' she fluted in pure top-drawer tones, gesturing towards the wellies – the significance of the connection between boots and cellar escaped me for the time being. I was swept through the enormous bare entrance hall and into the drawing room, a place of long-departed splendour where the carpets, curtains and upholstery were threadbare and faded to a uniform porridge shade. On taking the proffered seat, I was at once indecently assaulted by an errant spring; how, and

where, to sit on this furniture was only learned through painful experience. Tea was produced by a lady almost as old as Little Madam, clad in a wrap-over apron and the ubiquitous wellies, and the interview began. Not that it was really an interview, because we took to each other on sight. Anyone who can carry off a combination of diamonds and sacking with such panache is my kind of woman. Before the second cup of Lapsang had gone down the details had been settled; I would move in as soon as possible, would be completely responsible for all the food-shopping and cooking, would oversee the local ladies who came in and 'obliged', and could bring my cat with me. The wage was so small as to be almost non-existent, but I didn't even quibble; I was, after all, a rank tyro, and I would at least be fed and have a roof, of whatever quality, over my head. By the look of the rest of the house, a goodly supply of buckets and saucepans might well come in handy.

Suddenly Little Madam jumped to her feet with the sprightliness of someone half her age. Should we go to see my accommodation? It was not, she feared, frightfully well-equipped as it was furnished with stuff no longer fit for the main house. My heart quailed within me, having seen what *was* considered good enough. However, she went on, as far as heating went there was plenty of wood on the estate, and I had my own bathroom *and* an indoor lavatory. This last was, she obviously considered, an irresistible inducement. She led me through the classic 'green baize door' into the labyrinthine mysteries of below-stairs. We groped our way through dim uncarpeted corridors, past piles of mouldering wellies, croquet mallets, garden chairs, rusting lawnmowers, warped tennis racquets, shattered flower-pots, stacks of yellowing newspapers and heaps of unidentifiable *things*, through a scullery of incredible antiquity and stultifying cold, and up rickety stairs to a vast door.

'You have your *very own* front door,' explained Little Madam proudly, taking down a huge rusty key from a nail. She opened the door, not without difficulty, and the chill breath of the ages surged out at us. Extricating my foot from a wicker fishing-creel, I followed her in and down the gloomy corridor. 'Of course, no one's been living here for a while,' she went on, unnecessarily. 'My last lady didn't turn out to be suitable at all, I'm afraid; bit of a town bird, didn't like the country, too soft by half. Only a gel, though – no job for a gel, you know, needs a woman like yourself.' She flung open another door, 'Your sitting room!' she cried, and stood aside beaming all over her gentle face. I stepped in, looked round and with a mighty effort of will prevented my jaw hitting the floor. It was appalling. By comparison the drawing room had been the epitome of style and comfort. But such was Little Madam's charisma that I hadn't the heart to let her see what I thought of it. After all, I thought in desperation, I would be bringing some of my own stuff with me. And the sooner the better. There was a sofa with acute lordosis – the middle of the seat touched the floor – a bookcase leaned at a drunken angle against the wall, there was a massive Victorian wardrobe just made for bodies to tumble out of at a touch, an enormous iron fireplace containing a bird's nest complete with dead fledgling, a plastic-covered coffee table with a missing leg, and that was all. No carpet, no curtains, no chair. I swallowed, with an effort, several thousand misgivings and, turning to Little Madam, wrenched up a smile. 'I'll soon have it looking grand.'

Two weeks later, the move was complete. Cat and I were, if not cosily ensconced, at least installed. Cat adored it – acres of wild woods to desecrate; her evil little feline soul rejoiced as she became The Cat that Walks by Itself and also The Thing that Stalks by Night. A whole new side of her character appeared; daily offerings of mangled moles, mutilated mice and ravaged rabbits began to appear as she gave free rein to her previously-thwarted bloodlust, and no amount of smacks or scolding did any good at all. But her presence did help me to settle in, and I was very grateful for her warm little body on the bed beside me as I lay trying to sleep, listening to the wind howling in the tall trees and threatening to bring down the perilously unsafe chimneys through the sparsely slated roof.

For the first week or so I was more exhausted than I'd ever been in my life; my legs ached, my back ached, my hands were sore and my nails, never a strong point, were a truly horrid sight. The first few days were the worst. The kitchen, in keeping with the rest of the house, was totally devoid of mod. cons.; it was cavernous, stone-flagged, high-ceilinged, with a stone sink, a Neolithic refrigerator and a temperamental solid-fuel cooker, and I loved it. I couldn't wait to get into it in the mornings – mainly because it was warm, thanks to the cooker – and would plaster myself against the stove-front like Andromeda to the rock until I was thawed out sufficiently to dress. After I'd discovered that I was unlikely to be disturbed, I brought all my clothes in with me and put them in the oven to defrost, which was all right until the day I dressed hastily and later on the gardener retrieved a nicely browned bra from the oven where he'd been heating up his lunchtime pie. Despite the roaring wood fires which I lit in my room, at considerable risk to the chimney, my part of the house remained in a state of perma-frost, and at night I retired to bed clad fetchingly in long-johns, thick socks, flannel nightie, cardigan and, on really bad nights, woolly hat. Plus stone hot-water-bottle and, of course, Cat, who resented being clutched as a sort of supernumerary hottie and would inflict frantic scratches in her efforts to escape. I lived and slept in the sitting room – the bedroom was unusable – and after a while it did achieve a certain offbeat charm; there were so many rugs, shawls, blankets and pillows piled around in an effort to combat the piercing draughts that the place took on the air of a slightly raffish Turkish seraglio. Without, unfortunately, a slightly raffish Turkish pasha to complete the picture.

Little Madam was of the old English country-house school of upbringing; she considered heat unhealthy, comfort debilitating, and fresh, preferably freezing, air essential to the development of backbone, character and strength of will. She herself never seemed to feel the cold, insisting on her bedroom window being open all year round and her bed right up against it. Many's the time when I took up her morning tea, that I swear there was a small snowdrift on the bedspread. She allowed herself a modest log fire in the drawing room, which threw the heat all of two feet out into the room, scorching your shins and leaving your back freezing. The draughts whistled viciously through the old ill-fitting window frames, stirring her birds'-nest hair as she sat at a sensible distance from the fire – sensible to her way of thinking, that is, and about four feet further from the flames than I would have sat. I'd have been half-way up the chimney. A lifetime of such rigorous self-discipline had obviously paid off; she was well into her eighties, tiny, skinny and apparently frail, but she could walk me off my feet, hadn't seen a doctor since her babies were born half a century earlier, had her own teeth, didn't need glasses, and was out in all weathers, stumping round the wild neglected garden with secateurs and billhook waging vigorous war on the ever-encroaching nettles and brambles.

She was rarely without the wellies in which she had greeted me on the day of the interview, because she was rarely indoors and when she was she often went down into the cellar where, I discovered, they were essential. The whole house was slowly but surely sinking, and just as surely the water-table was rising in the cellars. The first time I went down there, in search of preserving jars, I stepped off the bottom step into ankle-deep water. It was a nasty shock, particularly as I was wearing the fluffy bedroom slippers on which I relied to combat the chill rising from the stone floor of the kitchen. Apparently there was nothing to be done to stem the flood, apart from the remote possibility of somehow jacking up the entire house; it seemed a terrible pity, as there was more stuff stored down there than in the passages and attics, much of it valuable and all of it gradually rotting away. In one cellar there were huge piles of pre-war magazines, transforming themselves by a process of osmosis into papier-mâché; I rescued as many as I could and spent many a happy hour huddled by my fire reading the latest news from Munich and tips on how to train the upstairs maid.

Fortunately for me, Little Madam ate like a bird – a wren rather than a vulture – and in line with the rest of her spartan philosophy, despised 'fancy food'. She was lovely and easy to cook for; boiled eggs, milk puddings, porridge, toast (burnt), rissoles, chops and plain boiled veg were all she asked for the entire time I was there. I think the most exotic item I ever produced was a cheese soufflé, and she didn't really approve; I think she felt it was almost degenerate. So it wasn't the cooking which made the place memorable; it was the sheer dottiness of the entire household. Little Madam may have been the only above-stairs resident, but a rich miscellany of others revolved around her like lesser planets around the sun. In the Good Old Days (to which she frequently referred, but never wistfully), there had been an indoor retinue of at least six, not counting ladies' maids and governess, and an outdoor staff of five permanent retainers plus seasonal casuals. Now there was me, two local ladies who obliged once a week each, one ancient gardener, and a character who was ostensibly the chauffeur – but as there was no longer a car, his duties were unspecified but seemed to embrace bringing in the logs, setting snares for the legions of rabbits (I lived in terror of Cat being caught in one), keeping the local hostelry's profits up, and keeping the female staff on their toes. He must have been a good seventy-five, but the fires of passion, unquenched, still stirred his ancient loins; no female from sixteen to seventy was safe from his enthusiastic advances. In all my years as a secretary, I'd never encountered the chase-round-the-desk cliché, but on my third day at Crumbling Court I found myself having to nip round the kitchen very smartish indeed, with Jack the Lad in hot pursuit. I was immensely grateful for the solid pine table, as well as the forty-odd years, that separated us as I evaded his attempts to do me 'a bit of good, me gal'. It was impossible to take offence, because he really couldn't understand how any woman could resist him, and right up to the day I left he was still determinedly seeking to arouse my lusts by such subtle overtures as offering to show me his giant marrow. His wife was a buxom woman, some thirty years his junior and twice his size, but she wore the permanently weary expression of one whose rest rarely went undisturbed.

The ladies who 'obliged' twice a week were wonderful gossips, treasure-houses of local information and scandal. My favourite time of the day, apart from when I fell prone onto my bed at night, was morning teatime when all staff in attendance that day, including the milkman if he could manage it, gathered round the kitchen table for umpteen cups of the lethally strong tea that stood stewing on the hotplate all day, and unlimited access to the biscuit tin. L.M. might have eaten frugally herself, but she never stinted the staff – one of my favourite, and most important, duties was keeping the biscuit and cake tins full for these occasions. While I sat preparing the latest batch of vegetables for freezer or lunch, Jack the Lad, Norman the ancient gardener, the milkman and the cleaning lady of the day would relax amid clouds of cigarette smoke while they regaled me with titbits of family history, ancient scandals and gruesome medical details. It was lovely and I took it all as gospel.

I learned all about the terrible time Mildred had with her third, why L.M.'s eldest son went to Australia so hurriedly, and why there was no photograph of the youngest daughter among the other family likenesses cluttering up the out-of-tune grand piano in the damp second drawing room. There was only one fuzzy snap of her, laughing in spotted beach-pyjamas and an ugly hat, in a little

heart-shaped silver frame by L.M.'s bed; she never told me who it was. But Mildred did. I also found out that Jack the Lad's amorous activities had been a feature of local life since time immemorial; there were, apparently, more than a few physical manifestations of his meanderings in the neighbourhood, ranging in age from over fifty to under six months. Perhaps in reprisal by the gods, he had no offspring born in wedlock – not his wedlock, anyway – which might have been another reason for his wife's air of weariness and her patient, uncomplaining acceptance of his wandering eye. He still chased Mildred and her co-worker Agnes when he got the chance, although I think more out of habit than anything else; Mildred told me he'd been chasing her since she was sixteen – half a century ago – but no amount of prodding over the teacups would elicit whether or not he had ever caught her. She would simply dissolve into shrill laughter and cries of 'Arr, that'd be tellin', wouldn't it?'

Norman, the gnome-like gardener, was another kettle of fish all together; he had been married for forty-five years to the same adored wife, and since she had died two years ago he found his only solace in the rambling kitchen garden and derelict greenhouses of Crumbling Court. Here he would grow only those things of which he himself approved; floury potatoes, giant carrots, marrows the size of barrage balloons, sprouts like tennis balls, beans a foot long. Attempts to get young tender vegetables out of him were doomed to failure. He defended his plants like a tigress her young until the produce reached what he considered the right size and was, in consequence, stringy, coarse and tasteless. I once tried to persuade him to grow courgettes and aubergines, but he dismissed them as flashy foreign rubbish and refused even to consider the idea. When, in self-defence against his favourite nondescript tomatoes, I raised a very special continental variety from seed, he deliberately forgot to water them while I was on holiday and they all perished. But he did grow the most marvellous soft fruit, which only got juicier and more luscious as it swelled; I have never eaten and cooked such delicious raspberries, strawberries, black, white and red currants and loganberries. And huge, smooth, purple dessert gooseberries, warm from the sun, bursting in the mouth with a winey fragrance. Plus, on a south wall, an ancient fig tree which produced every season no more than half a dozen perfect, succulent, wickedly decadent fruit. They were the only thing he cultivated that he didn't like; but the tree had been there even longer than he had. Each fig, as it reached perfection, he gently picked and brought to L.M. as one might bring a jewel to a princess and she, fully appreciative of the solemnity of the occasion, would first admire it and then, slowly and luxuriously, eat it there and then. It was about the only luxury in which I ever saw her indulge.

Despite the general simplicity of her tastes, cooking for L.M. was not without its hazards, most of them caused by a combination of inexperience, blind panic and sheer incompetence. I had cooked perfectly adequately for my own family for years – but it had *been* my own, and any disasters could be countered by a terse 'Eat it, or go without', or by the simple expedient of flinging the offending item into the luckless dog's dish and resorting to egg and chips, which the children liked better anyway. (It was a great bone of contention between us that, after carefully raising my children on a diet of Italian, Greek, French, Chinese and Indian food, they far preferred regular British fry-ups and fish fingers. No doubt, had I dragged them up on doorsteps of bread and dripping, they'd all have turned out Cordon Bleu cooks by the age of ten.) Cooking for someone else, for money, was a different matter all together – I could hardly bully L.M. into eating up her charred chop or burnt semolina pudding by threatening her with early bed and no story. She was immensely patient with all my mistakes, however, even the worst; the coffee pot delivered plus coffee but minus water would simply be handed back with a gentle, apologetic 'No water, dear,' while the Orange Delight cooked for one of her rare supper parties, which reached the table resembling a ceiling tile (I had made the elementary mistake of putting it in the oven before the first course went in, instead of waiting to see how long they would take), was pronounced 'Perhaps not *quite* a delight, dear, but nonetheless *delicious*.' Whether the guests, chewing their way manfully through bright yellow polystyrene, were of the same opinion is anyone's guess; they couldn't get their teeth apart long enough to pass any comment.

She rose to her greatest heights of tolerance, however, on The Night the Table Fell In. Again, it was a gala occasion; several of her children, plus the local vicar and his wife, were invited to dinner and accordingly the extension flap had to be inserted into the dining-table. Caught up in all the fuss of cooking, doing the flowers, setting the table with the family silver and ensuring that I selected the least tattered of the table linen, I somehow overlooked the essential step of inserting the little pegs that supported the extension. The table held up bravely until the main course was halfway consumed when, laden to its limit with food, silver, flowers, wine-glasses and elbows as the guests leaned over the table in excited argument (L.M.'s children were extremely voluble, like their mother), the whole middle section collapsed, with an agonised groan, on to the floor while I was helping the vicar to carrots. I was shattered and so were three wine-glasses, a tureen of potatoes, a sideplate and what I still fear was a Ming vase, full of peonies. I disappeared under the table in short order and was scrabbling desperately about on hands and knees gathering up beans, potatoes, shards of glass and porcelain and my wits when L.M. merely leaned down and, hardly pausing in mid-forkful, whispered, 'Never mind, dear, we'll just carry on with our conversation and pretend it didn't

21

happen.' And she did, sweeping the other guests along with her, so that I was able to crawl out and find the supports while the guests, without breaking the flow of their discussion, held the table up with their knees until I could insert the little brass bits. She never mentioned the incident afterwards, and I saw what made ladies of her class and generation able to travel the world and face the worst the locals could throw at them.

Despite the sadly depleted family fortune, there were two things L.M. did spend money on – oilpaints and canvases. Painting was her greatest pleasure, and she spent hours, even in snowy weather, sitting in the woods or on the hill in the biting wind, plonked firmly on her camp-stool in front of the easel, her legs planted solidly apart exposing yards of beige directoire knicker and well-darned lisle stockings, spiralling round her legs. Her paintings, to be honest, were not very good; she had received the usual Victorian young lady's artistic education and was technically competent, but not especially gifted. She gave me a little painting as a Christmas present, of a vase of holly and stiff Christmas roses, and I wouldn't part with it for the world.

Because she was so strict with herself and never got so much as a cold – 'a good walk and some deep breathing, dear, and you'll never get a cold' was her advice when I was dropping with the flu – we never expected her to be ill, or get older, or change in any way at all. Indeed, I couldn't imagine her ever having been any different from the way she was and when she showed me ancient sepia photographs of herself as a young girl, in her Prince of Wales ostrich feathers, it was hard to connect the two. So it was a terrible shock when, coming back on duty one afternoon after my two-hour break, I went through the hall with the tea tray and found her lying at the foot of the stairs. She had caught her foot in the threadbare staircarpet and fallen down twelve steps, landing hard on her side on the wooden floor. She was just conscious but very cold and must have been lying there quite some time. 'Just a bang, dear, so silly,' she said faintly; but when I tried to move her her face went even whiter. The doctor arrived within minutes of my call and examined her there on the hall floor, where I had tried to make her a little more comfortable with pillows and the picnic rug.

Her hip, and three ribs, were badly broken, and her stay in hospital was a long one; at her age bones didn't mend very quickly, or very satisfactorily. With her away the house was silent and depressing; I found it quite frightening and hated going upstairs to put away the laundry or air the rooms. Once or twice, doing some job in the bedrooms or on the echoing landing under the gloomy old family portraits, I turned round suddenly and had the unnerving feeling that if I'd been just a fraction quicker, I'd have seen whoever it was that was watching me. The tail of my eye seemed to have caught a movement, something or someone slipping behind a door or through a mirror. Perhaps they were shadows that L.M. knew and loved, but without her down-to-earth, no-nonsense presence in the house, it was very easy to get fanciful, especially at night when the nearest living soul was Norman the gardener in his cottage five hundred yards away through the woods. I locked myself in my rooms with Cat for comfort, with the television turned up very loudly to hide the noises and a glass of the old and fruity to make me brave. Once, Jack the Lad, going home after a nocturnal check on his snares, tapped on the window to enquire if I was all right and I nearly died of fright. Thank heavens he didn't fancy his chances that night – it was probably too cold – because in the state I was in, I couldn't have fought off Norman the Gnome, let alone the Demon Daddy of Derbyshire.

For weeks and weeks I held the fort. I spent my days preparing and blanching vast quantities of fruit and vegetables with which I rather pointlessly filled the freezer, reading, visiting the hospital and avoiding going into the main house alone, and my evenings being deafened by the television, clutching Cat and anaesthetising myself with alcohol so that I could go to bed at nine o'clock and the night would be over more quickly. It's a wonder I didn't become seriously addicted. Lurching into the lovely safe kitchen in the mornings, groggy with sherry-induced sleep, I would fling my knickers into the slow oven and grope my way to the tap to fill the kettle for a mouth-unglueing cup of tea. Then, sitting with my feet in the warming drawer and gulping the life-giving fluid, I would hug the comforting thought that another night was over and tell myself that, once L.M. came home, everything would be back to normal.

(Ridiculous, that the presence of one tiny old lady five minutes away at the other end of the house should have made such a difference; but it did.) But that wasn't to be; the doctors decided that, even with the resident nurse that she couldn't afford, there was no way that she could return to the rigours of life at Crumbling Court.

On the day she told me of the doctors' verdict, for the only time I saw her iron self-discipline waver. Age, pain and helplessness had taken their toll, and she wept. But only for a moment, then while my heart still ached for her, she blew her nose crossly on her large sensible handkerchief and patted my hand. 'Sorry, my dear, so silly of me,' she said. 'My daughter has a simply lovely room ready, I shall be as snug as could be' – snug? she who scorned the creature comforts? – 'it's on the ground floor and I'll be able to look out over the garden.' It was almost too much. I knew her daughter's house and it was indeed comfortable – on an executive estate with manicured, sensibly-sized back gardens and open-plan frontages. I thought of L.M.s view from the drawing room at home – riots of naturalised daffodils, ancient lilac and magnolia trees, wistaria and clematis clambering, unpruned, through the old trees, honeysuckle and japonica, snowdrops and primroses, winter jasmine, roses in profusion, and everywhere, the long grass and wild flowers that were no longer kept at bay by an army of gardeners. And rabbits, and squirrels, and birds . . .

The house and grounds were sold to developers, and I was glad L.M. was unlikely ever to visit the site and see what had happened to it. I never went back myself, it would have been too painful. L.M. was deeply concerned over what would become of all the staff, and went to great lengths to see that everyone was looked after. Norman, Jack the Lad, Mildred and Agnes were, of course, all well past retirement age, but the two men had lived in rent-free cottages in the grounds. From the proceeds of the sale, freehold houses in the village were bought for both of them, small, but with such exotic modern luxuries as indoor sanitation and hot-water systems, things without which they had previously managed quite happily. Mildred and Agnes, as old part-time retainers, found the freeholds of their houses bought for them, plus, in gratitude for their years of cheerful, slapdash help, a little personal cheque each which caused Agnes to burst into joyful tears and not only at the prospect of at long last being able to visit her daughter in New Zealand. I had only been a member of the 'family' for just over a year but L.M. was concerned for me too and pressed me to stay at Crumbling Court, on the payroll, until I found another job that I really liked. But I'd had enough; the good days were gone, and I arranged to go and stay with a friend while I perused the sits. vac. columns of the *Lady* and the *Telegraph*.

Before leaving I went to say goodbye to L.M., now settled in her pleasant daughter's pleasant house a mile or two away; she was sitting bolt upright in a chair by the window, her despised but necessary walking-stick propping the window open further than it was supposed to go. She had her easel set up, and was well away on a painting of the view. She greeted me affectionately, and we chatted for a while about our plans – she was going to do a series of paintings of the garden in all four seasons – when she suddenly clutched my arm and pointed out of the window. 'Look, a squirrel!' And so there was, sitting up with its paws held before its face. I felt much happier all of a sudden. As I left, promising to keep in touch, she offered her crumpled-silk cheek to be kissed, and gave me a package from beside her chair. 'Just a little keepsake, dear,' she said. 'It was such a happy time when you were with me. Open it when you get home.'

It contained a letter, in her beautiful copper-plate hand-writing, asking me to keep in touch and thanking me for everything I'd done; a reference, in glowing terms of such sincerity that I think, on the strength of it, St Peter would have made me heaven's housekeeper without hesitation; and an old silver heart-shaped photograph frame.

Full of Eastern Promise

Until I had started reading the columns of the magazines and newspapers which catered for those in the fortunate position of being able to employ domestic help, I hadn't realised just how many there actually were. Obviously a complete section of society still existed in which people wouldn't dream of doing their own cooking, cleaning, laundry, childraising and gardening, and what's more could afford to pay someone else to cope with all the basic unpleasantnesses of life. While I, in common with the herd, was struggling along in the everyday world where a full-time outside job had to be managed as well as all the household chores, where wives trudged round supermarkets dragging reluctant toddlers and recalcitrant pushchairs, or carried huge unwieldy bundles of laundry to the launderette, there was a whole other world of women who had never washed a nappy in their lives, had never walked the floor with a fretful baby, never scratched the solidified porridge from the saucepan with their nails, never coped with smelly socks or the squalid aftermath of a dinner party. And yet they were always busy – one saw them in the glossy magazines, attending horse-trials or art-gallery openings, at hunt balls and cocktail parties, at first nights and garden parties and posh weddings and society christenings and coming-of-age parties and engagements. No wonder they never got round to cleaning the oven or unbunging the drains. They just hadn't the time!

I sometimes used to wonder how they found time to bear their own children and in fact knew quite a few who found it all 'a frightful bore', particularly if the unavoidable few days of confinement coincided with Henley or Derby Day – if only Nanny could have been persuaded to be a true surrogate mother . . .

(Sometimes it was pure good luck that Nanny wasn't; there were plenty of Sirs who didn't confine their attentions to their respective legal Madams.)

Having had my first housekeeping experience with L.M., I thought in my innocence that all employers were modelled along the same lines; I should have known better, and soon did. For the first few weeks of my unwanted freedom, I wrote letters in response to every advertisement that seemed even vaguely attractive, from cook-general to children's nanny, but somehow not one of them appealed to me after the interview. True, most of them offered considerably better living conditions than I had become used to, but there were definite drawbacks; some wanted Cordon Bleu cooks at Mrs Beeton prices, some had the most appalling offspring, some spent their time zipping back and forth from town house to country seat with the concomitant constant packing and unpacking. Some were downright rude, and one or two – single gentlemen living alone – obviously expected more for their money than just housekeeping. If I was going to warm anyone's bed, it would be purely as a bonus – and in any case, those who made it clear that they expected extra services were hardly the sort to send a girl wild with desire . . .

Before long, I was getting a bit desperate; money was getting very scarce indeed, and the long-suffering friend with whom I'd been staying since leaving Crumbling Court, keen to have the flat to herself and her multifarious boyfriends, took to dropping subtle hints like 'When on earth are you going to move out?' Cat too was starting to feel the strain; there was a canary in a cage on the piano, and the constant frustration of being batted off the piano with a tennis racquet every time she launched an attack was telling on her nerves. Not to mention the canary's. I began to feel that I'd just have to take the first job that was offered, no matter what as long as I could take Cat with me, when I spotted The Advertisement.

It sounded perfect. 'Caretaker-cook for large house in Wimbledon. Owner rarely in residence, occasionally visits with son. Highest wages paid; highest references essential.' Easy-peasy! There'd be thousands after it! Quickly, before it was snatched from under my very nose, I telephoned the number given, and an appointment was made for an interview with the owner's lawyers; he himself was out of the country. The lawyers' secretary sounded terrifyingly elegant, her accent so plummy as to almost unintelligible; I dressed with great care and some trepidation; this was obviously not the occasion for the humble cross-over crimplene or the shabby-genteel navy mac. I lashed out some of my last few quid on a hairdo; it would never do to attend this  essential interview with my hair in its usual hennaed havoc. Clad in my one and only good black afternoon dress, plain black courts, dark tights and my precious skunk coat – legacy of a brief but glorious period of my life when I'd had some money – I literally went to town, in a taxi.

The interview went like a dream; L.M.'s reference, plus another wrested from my friend by the promise of unlimited borrowing rights over the skunk, seemed to impress tremendously. (Would that employers were similarly called upon to provide references; you never find out until it's too late.) I was given tea in bone china, and the sort of biscuits I'd only previously encountered in Fortnum and Mason's window, and the details of the job. The owner of the house was from the East, very well-connected and enormously wealthy – hence the close investigation into applicants' backgrounds – and he would rarely, if ever, be in London. When he was, he would usually be alone. Occasionally, he might be accompanied by his eldest son. But the main burden of the job – burden? I thought – would be to look after his house, keep it clean, aired and secure, and oversee the gardener. The wages were high. And so, although I didn't know it then, was the cost.

The interview went so well that, filled with euphoric optimism, I took a taxi home, too. They were going to get in touch with me as soon as all the necessary ferreting had been completed; I prayed that they wouldn't find out anything too damning in my past, like the Mars bar I shoplifted from Woolies when I was eight. The suspense of the next week was awful; I practically hi-jacked the postman every morning, and leapt like a startled stag every time the phone rang. At last a letter, on thick, cream-laid paper, arrived; I hid in the hall cupboard to open it, lest it was a rejection, and when I saw what it said I burst out of the cupboard like an Apache out of ambush, knocking my friend clear into the umbrella-stand and scaring Cat, who was scaling the south col of the piano again, clear out of her wits. The job was mine!

Overjoyed at securing this heavenly sinecure in the face of what I was sure must have been tremendous competition, I moved into the mansion. And mansion it was; beautifully furnished, exquisitely decorated, lavishly fitted with all a cook-housekeeper could desire. The kitchen was larger than my entire quarters at Crumbling Court; the pantry, replete with fridges and freezers, would have housed a regiment. My own apartment was a slight comedown after all this glory; admittedly it had a sitting room, kitchenette, bathroom and bedroom, but if I had a visitor we would have to take it in turns to breathe. Still, it was nicely, if plainly, furnished, and I wouldn't have to pay for my heating or lighting. What I didn't realise was how little time I'd spend in it – all that was really necessary was a bed, placed conveniently just inside the door for falling into in a stupor of exhaustion.

But the first two weeks were blissful. I had the place to myself, and indulged in a way of life utterly foreign to me and to which, unfortunately, I was not to become accustomed. I rose late, did a little light dusting, cooked delectable little meals for myself and Cat, sunbathed in the garden, and explored the house exhaustively from attics to cellars. There was a well-stocked wine cellar which, with commendable willpower, I did not broach, contenting myself with the wide range of mineral waters in the enormous fridge. Then, just as I was getting used to being a sybarite, a message arrived from The Office in The City – the boss was on his way. Mr B was a Big Businessman, although I never did discover what his business was – one thing was certain, it was highly profitable.

I filled the house with fresh flowers, changed out of the bikini in which I had lived for the past fortnight into my uniform overall, locked Cat, protesting, into my flatlet and stood on the front step, the picture of the efficient, welcoming housekeeper. The Daimler swept up to the door and out stepped Mr B. Not alone, as expected, but accompanied by two sons, one daughter, two grandchildren and a butler . . . My carefully planned menu for one was going to have to be drastically stretched. It was my first – but by no means my last – encounter with the unexpected, and my first experience of coping with it. It wasn't easy.

The thing that struck me most of all was the sheer *volume* of food that I had to provide; meals had to be at least twice as large as could possibly be consumed, and vast quantities must be carried out of the dining room at the end of each session. My essentially frugal nature found this hard to endure, but apparently it was all to do with status; the more food displayed, the better. Nor was I encouraged to transform the rejects into made-up dishes; what happened to the leftovers was of no interest to my employers, and for the first and (I regretfully suspect) the last time in my life I got literally fed-up with fillet steaks, strawberries, whipped cream, asparagus, smoked salmon . . . The memory makes me drool. Many's the time I tottered up to bed so full I could hardly breathe; an upbringing in which the starving hordes of China had been cited every time a scrap was left on the plate was taking its toll. It took ages after we left before Cat stopped turning up her nose at anything other than smoked salmon scraps, garnished with caviare.

In return for this rich diet, however, I had to learn tricks of the catering trade previously unknown to me. Quite often, dinner would be ordered for, say, eight o'clock for, say, ten people. I would go into a frenzy of activity in the kitchen; artichokes would be stuffed with soufflé, a dozen choice fillet steaks would be at the point of perfection, delicate desserts would be approaching their moment of triumph, rare vegetables awaiting their baptism of butter and herbs. Then, just as I was about to despatch the butler to beat the gong, a figure would appear in the doorway – usually one of the sons – and announce casually, 'We're going out. We will have dinner at ten instead. There will be two more guests,' and disappear. Collapse of soufflés, stout party (the butler), and anguished cook.

The butler and I would sit down and disconsolately stuff ourselves with the unsalvagable parts of the meal, after which I would struggle frantically, with much cursing and swearing, to maintain what food I could in an appetising condition and replace the rest. It was enough to break the spirit of any self-respecting cook. Fortunately the butler turned out to be a great comfort; he was one of the old school, very British, very correct, and subtly corrupt. He was in charge of the wine cellar, and was adept at keeping us both adequately and unsuspectedly supplied; many's the bottle of cook's comfort and butler's bonus we shared over the mangled remnants of dinner.

Mr B, being a devout man, merely stocked liquor for his guests, he did not take it himself; nor did any of his family – while he was in residence. It was a rather different matter, however, when the sons were staying alone in the house. Their religious scruples restrained them not at all, and every evening saw a lavish and riotous dinner party at which the guests seemed to consist mainly of a great many very brightly coloured ladies, of impeccable accent but not so peccable morals. I learned to ignore the giggles and shrieks and bumps that echoed through the house once I had staggered exhausted to bed in the small hours, and I could now see some point in the tiresome ritual of changing every item of bed-linen daily. I also began to appreciate why strict honesty had figured so large in the lawyers' investigations; huge bundles of notes and piles of silver were left on dressing tables, in suits left out for cleaning, in bathrooms, on coffee tables. When the daughters came to stay, stray jewellery also lay about in profusion; diamond rings in soapdishes, emerald necklaces tossed into corners, sapphire earrings in the strangest places.

One daughter in particular was a very sweet girl, whose whole existence was devoted to spending money; she explained that she had to have a constant supply of new clothes, as having worn something once 'out' and once 'at home', it was no longer of any use. 'Old' clothes – twice-worn Zandra Rhodes creations, Jap outfits seen on her by as many as three people – were bundled up and sent back home for the poor relations. I had visions of little old ladies toiling in the sun, clad in the glory that was St Laurent. Once, as I was helping her to cram the Vuitton luggage for a flight home, I noticed, lying in the middle of the bedroom floor, two beautiful pairs of Italian leather boots, one black, one tan. Did she want me to pack them? No, she said, they were worn out, but she would wear one pair on the plane and discard them on arrival. I inspected the boots. They were slightly down at the heels. Should I, perhaps, have the other pair mended and send them on? Shock at the very idea flitted over her pretty face – no, no, just throw them away. She dragged on the black boots and I followed her downstairs, waved goodbye and then, as the car disappeared, regained the bedroom with a turn of speed worthy of Seb Coe for fear that someone might

31

have got there before me. All was well – the tan boots were still there! But not for long. In seconds I was in my room, pulling them on with fevered haste. They fitted perfectly. Even if they'd crippled me, I'd have suffered gladly. I had them heeled, and I have them still, my lovely Italian boots. She also left a fabulous Bill Gibb evening dress hanging in the wardrobe, but discretion dictated that I left that untouched; after all, she hadn't actually said she didn't want it, and you never know – the traditional punishment for petty thefts in those parts might have resulted. A cook-housekeeper missing the odd hand could have a hard time of it.

Next to this daughter, my favourite guest was the ancient auntie who was brought over to see a specialist. Unlike the younger members of the family, she was quite un-Westernised, and spent her entire visit sitting on a rug in her room, draped in black. She knew no English and we communicated by signs, smiles and touches. I rounded up every picture-book I could find, including some left over from my children's youth, and she spent many a delightful hour poring over *Bunty* and *Eagle* annuals, *Mother Goose's Nursery Rhymes*, *The Illustrated Home Doctor* and *1000 Things a Girl Can Do* (none of them interesting unless you wanted to make a

flowerpot out of a gramophone record). She wouldn't allow me to touch her laundry; instead she festooned her bathroom with enormous, dripping-wet, black knickers every day – the only washing she seemed to do all the time she was there. When she left, she called me in and pressed twenty pounds into my hand, smiling and nodding. I was very touched.

Eventually the flood of visitors became more than I could handle;

the house was never empty and I was cooking, washing-up and making beds for what seemed like twenty-three out of the twenty-four hours of the day. Through a fog of exhaustion, I petitioned Mr B to see if it were possible for a specific number of hours a day to be fixed. This met with fierce disapproval and I was told that all the English were the same, all they thought about was their free time; why, at home the servants slept across the bedroom doorways, happy and grateful to be of service at any hour of the day and night. But the English . . . why, they even wanted holidays! Biting back the temptation to rush to my countrymen's and women's defence, I pointed out the original terms of employment – but to no avail. I was ungrateful and unappreciative; they did, did they not, allow me Sunday afternoon and evening off, and serve their own supper on that day? With an effort, I forbore from mentioning the amount of work involved in providing said supper and cleaning up afterwards, first thing on Monday morning. It would have done no good, and could have led to even more unpleasantness. I quietly made up my mind to look for somewhere else, and left the room, wondering if I should, perhaps, do so on hands and knees.

Soon afterwards I answered an advertisement for a position as cook-housekeeper with another upper-class English lady – what a contrast, I thought, what a change, what a *rest* – a small house in Little Venice, no children, it should be bliss . . .

The Dogs of Venice

This time the advertisement had been placed by an agency, and when I reached their office they positively leapt at me. I just thought they'd recognised a pearl beyond price; the idea that their enthusiastic welcome might have been motivated by desperation never crossed my mind. The interview this time was brief – a quick flash of the references, a few questions about my previous experience (hardly impressive), and I was despatched post-haste to see Mrs X after having been most warmly recommended to her over the phone. I wondered how they could know how super I was on such short acquaintance: to listen to them, you'd have thought they'd known me for years.

I decided against the skunk this time, and settled for the neat-but-not-gaudy, including a sensible hat and flat shoes. The wage offered, although good, was not exceptional, and I didn't feel that overkill was necessary; I didn't want to look too expensive, just worthy and honest. Mrs X herself let me in, a solidly-built woman, heavily made up and dressed in classic Sloane Ranger style. The house was absolutely lovely; a little jewel box in exquisite taste, filled with carefully tended antiques and un-threadbare Persian carpets – a complete contrast to the loved shabbiness of Crumbling Court and the flash of the Middle East. I was offered a glass of sherry, which I accepted with alacrity – just as well, as it was the last I ever got. Mrs X, all smiles, told me she was very easy to work for, as long as (this was ominous) her staff were reasonable. A maid came in to do the 'rough', and apart from that there would be only the cooking and daily dusting. She herself did the food shopping. Terrific, I thought; no more dragging back from the shops with bags of groceries, my arms stretched down to my ankles. As for the dusting, it would be a walk-over; even at my speed I could nip round such a small establishment in under an hour a day. I was escorted round; upstairs, downstairs and in my lady's chamber, which had very pretty blue-silk draped walls and promised to be a real dust-trap. This time there was a Mr X in residence too; he dealt in antiques and had his own rooms, very masculine and filled with silver trophies which I hoped came under the heading of 'rough'.

There was only one drawback – over the entire house hung an all-pervading odour of Dog. And when we reached the nether regions, the source became clear – lying on the rug in the basement kitchen were no fewer than five very small, very hairy and extremely malodorous canines of uncertain ancestry and very little im-mediately obvious charm. They leapt upon Mrs X with shrill vociferous clamourings, and I thought of Cat and her blood lust. She'd have them for breakfast, if they didn't gang up on her first. Interrupting Mrs X's flow of extravagant endearments to the animated floor mops, I hesitantly informed her of the existence of Cat, and how she was my prop, stay and fairly constant companion. A look of sheer disgust appeared on her face – which I thought a bit much, considering how cleverly I'd disguised my own feelings at the sight of her menagerie – and, scooping up an armful of assorted dog, she announced that the presence of Cat would be absolutely Out Of The Question. Cats, she went on hootingly, were not only filthy in their personal habits (I hastily averted my gaze from the activities of two of the heaving horde), but were in addition sly, cruel, untrustworthy and lacking in affection. No one, but *no one*, could prefer them to dogs, as she was sure I would agree once I came to know and love her own dear brood.

Now I have never been one for dogs – all right in their place, which is preferably outdoors, doubtless useful in their way and probably a very welcome sight if you are up to your neck in snow on the St Gotthard Pass, but for everyday sensible companionship your cat is the answer. It's the fawning on anyone misguided enough to encourage them that puts me off with dogs; cats, on the other hand, bestow their affection only when they feel it's merited, and no amount of flattery will win it against their inclination. However, this was a problem which would have to be surmounted; love me, love my cat, and if Mrs X wanted the benefit of my master-touch with the frying pan, some arrangement would have to be made to accommodate Cat too. For my part, I would somehow have to come to terms with the presence of the hairy horrors. If everything else was acceptable in the job, perhaps I could accept them too, or at least try to ignore them. I hoped they usually lived upstairs.

Mrs X obviously *was* keen to secure my doubtful talents. A compromise was reached; Cat could come, provided she was confined to my rooms in the basement and never allowed into the rest of the house. As for the dogs, I need not worry; she herself prepared their food, groomed and exercised them, and if their presence in the kitchen was a nuisance I was free to eject them – although, she reiterated, she was sure that I would soon be as fond of them as she was herself. Eyeing the little beasts, one of which was attempting to seduce the table leg, I doubted it strongly. But I'd cross that bridge when I came to it; I needed the job, it didn't look as if it would be too onerous, and when a firm offer was made I accepted.

Once again I packed up my books, my clothes and Cat, and installed everything in a new home. This time it comprised a basement flat of two rooms, a little dark but, in common with the rest of the house, nicely decorated and furnished. No more hitting the floor when I sat on the sofa; and enough room, this time, to stretch my legs. I looked forward to seeing more of my own flat than I had in the previous job and to making it a real home rather than just a place to sleep. And indeed, it did become a pleasant haven; but unfortunately the lay-out was such that through my sitting room was the quickest route from the garage to the kitchen, and I first made the acquaintance of the chauffeur clad in knickers and bra. Me, not him. He didn't turn a hair; he simply marched through, elegant in maroon uniform, gleaming gaiters and cap, which he tipped to me politely as I stood, stunned, by the ironing board. I was grateful that I had on the sensible British Home Stores underwear and not the Janet Reger; it would have been wasted on him. Pity, really; in other circumstances, or with the next-door chauffeur who, if I left off my glasses and squinted a bit, almost resembled Paul Newman, it might have been very different . . .

The maid who came to do the 'rough' was Italian, very pretty, very friendly and with hardly any English; we got on terrifically in a mixture of sign-language and pidgin-Italian and English. She had been working there for more than a year and was no fonder of the

dogs than when she first started. 'Feelthy! All dogs mocky!' she would cry in disgust as we gingerly cleared their leavings from nooks and crannies all over the house – they were highly-strung and any stress went immediately to the bowels. They slept wherever they would, including in the beds; Gina put on rubber gloves when she helped me change the sheets because of the hairs and what the advertisements euphemistically call 'understains'. She would push the dogs out of the way when she was cleaning, hissing 'Outta da way, outta da way – you meck mock, I keel you,' as she drove at them with the vacuum cleaner. They would yelp and snap at the machine, and several times she very nearly sucked one up the tube. The whole lot of them were obsessed by sex and the fact that they were all male made no difference at all; they assaulted each other with the same impartial enthusiasm which they displayed towards chair legs, table legs and human legs. But despite the manifest unpleasantness of their behaviour and appearance, Mrs X loved them besottedly; somewhere out in the world she had children, but they came very far down her list of priorities. The Dogs came first. Mr X came a very poor second, if not third; there was, after all, her Bridge, as well.

She was true to her word as far as feeding the brutes went. Every day she would descend to the cell-like basement kitchen (there were even bars on the window) to prepare their dinner. This took her hours and while she was there I couldn't get on with whatever I was doing. She sat at the table, carefully cutting up the very best quality beef, chicken or liver into minute particles before mixing it with vitamins, minerals, puppy biscuit and, probably, aphrodisiacs. Then this mixture would be ceremoniously ladled out into five individual bowls each bearing the name of its owner and put down on the floor right where it was most inconvenient. The Hounds of the Baskervilles would be let in, five seconds of chaos would ensue, and the bowls would be clean as a whistle. 'They *do* appreciate it,' she would smile, surveying the mob as they rushed madly to and fro investigating each other's bowls. 'They know their mother only gives them the best.' Having witnessed their equally consuming appetite for far less salubrious items, some of them unmentionably disgusting, I knew they didn't give a tinker's cuss whether it was 'the best' or not; they would eat anything and frequently did. Unlike Cat who, if the proffered food were not up to her exacting standard, would walk away with an expression of withering scorn and starve rather than touch it . . .

But one thing was certain; the food provided for the canine delinquents was of a considerably higher quality than that provided for the household's humans. My relief at finding that I wouldn't have to do the food shopping was short-lived. No longer could I, in time-honoured domestic-staff tradition, strike comfortable little bargains with butchers, fishmongers and the like, such as a tasty bit of steak for myself or an extra slice of halibut for Cat added to the family bill. From the £200 a week housekeeping which I had to play with in my last job, I was down to nothing; no chance of buying the fruit in a Soho street-market instead of Harrods and pocketing the difference; no chance of you-scratch-my-back-and-I'll-scratch-yours with the grocer. I could have done without the perks, but it didn't stop there. Not to put too fine a point on it, Mrs X was Close. It was a constant challenge to meet her standards on the food provided, and one which I wasn't always up to meeting. She entertained fairly frequently, but her ideas of party food were not mine; I had hoped for more exciting tasks than making casseroles (without wine – too expensive, without garlic – too smelly) and stewed fruit.

One particular dinner party was particularly trying to cater for. She had ordered vichyssoise, followed by roast chicken and (greatly daring!) caramelised oranges. The day before the dinner, she departed in the Rolls, complete with chauffeur and dogs, to lay in the necessaries. A couple of hours later she returned and swept down the stairs to the kitchen, where I was gloomily defrosting fishcakes for supper. 'There,' she trumpeted triumphantly. 'A leek for the vichyssoise!' Somewhat taken aback, I surveyed the one small leek and ventured the opinion that perhaps, as there were to be eight guests, one leek might be cutting it a bit fine. Nonsense, she said, one would be ample; after all, it was only for flavouring. And ample it had to be – but vichyssoise it was not. (But although I say it as shouldn't, it was excellent *potato soup*.)

She had also purchased the chicken, and once again had not exactly gone over-board. I gazed at the poor starveling that lay, legs in air, on the kitchen table. It resembled nothing so much as a malnourished budgie. Tentatively, I suggested sausages, bacon rolls and stuffing to help it along but she remained adamant. The bird alone, with two veg, and bread sauce, would be perfectly adequate. Never have I cooked a chicken with such slow, tender, loving care; I was terrified lest it shrink even more. But despite my efforts, when I finally bore it shamefacedly into the dining room it still looked lost on the silver platter. Even the jungle of watercress could do nothing to disguise it. The guests must have found it less than satisfying too, because when I cleared the plates the very bones were gnawed; I hurled them into the bin under the sink and emptied the sink-tidy on top, to hide the pitiful sight.

No sooner had the guests departed, no doubt making for the nearest chippie, than Mrs X descended trailing clouds of glory and a strong aroma of gin. She did not congratulate me on my conjuring tricks with the dinner; that wasn't her style and in any case the meal was hardly cause for congratulation. Instead, she enquired as to the whereabouts of the tiny carcase. 'In the bin,' I said. 'What!' – I thought she would explode – 'take those bones out at once! You can make two good bowls of jellied stock from them.' Appalled, I pointed out that they were not only picked clean, but liberally decorated with coffee grounds, potato peelings and fag ends. 'A quick boil will kill off the germs,' she bellowed, diving for the bin; and, opening the lid, she bade me delve in, hoick them out and rinse them off. The two bowls of Good Jellied Stock must be forthcoming, or heaven help me. Of course they were, but it wasn't heaven that helped me; it was half the packet of powdered gelatine.

On another occasion, my mother came to stay for a day or two as a sort of grace and favour. (It wasn't said in as many words, but I inferred that, if she didn't do something to earn her keep, I'd never hear the end of it; so she dusted a bit and yelled at the dogs for me.) On the last day of the visit, Mrs X came sweeping down the stairs with a small brown paper bag extended elegantly at arm's length. 'I've brought a little treat for your mother,' she intoned graciously, as one taking soup to the cottagers. 'I know how fond she is of them.' Repressing an urge to curtsey, mother took the bag and opened it eagerly. A pineapple? A mango, perhaps? Or even an avocado? No such luxury. It was a tomato . . .

This carefulness did not, however, extend to the drinks department; my employer was very fond of a wee dram and didn't stint herself. As the evening wore on, her descent of the kitchen stairs was inclined to be more and more unsteady, and more than once she made the entire journey on her back, whereupon she would pick herself up, glare fiercely at the stairs and declare, 'Must have tripped on something – you *must* keep those stairs clear', in a voice less than usually coherent. Sunday was her best day, especially in good weather when lunch would be served in the garden; many's the Sunday morning, slaving over a hot stove to reproduce the miracle of the loaves and fishes, that I gazed out of the window to see her, brimming champagne glass in hand, swanning round the flowerbeds like a female version of Kenny Everett's Hooray Henry. And I didn't even have any cooking sherry with which to console myself. I began to understand how cooks can become addicted to the vanilla essence.

All in all, though, it wasn't too bad a life. I was near the heart of London, I had a day and a half off a week and the work wasn't arduous, nothing like the non-stop entertaining and housework of my previous position. Cat didn't like it much, though; she hated the smell of the dogs everywhere (an aversion we shared) and it annoyed her that she wasn't allowed into the garden. She would crouch on the windowsill, gazing out at passing birds and dogs, growling and yattering furiously because they were so near and yet so far. I lived in dread that she would slip out one day when the chauffeur was taking one of his short cuts, and the dogs would set on her; one at a time she could have picked them off easily, but not mob-handed.

Nevertheless, I might have stayed on long enough to become an Old Retainer; Gina was good company, and the house was so pretty and pleasant, apart from the pong, and it was too much effort to start looking for somewhere else. Better the devil you knew, I thought, every time thoughts of revolt surfaced. But gradually, Mrs X began extending my duties into realms which were definitely not my responsibility. Ladies' maiding, for instance, was not within my terms of employment, but items of mending started being handed over to me – buttons on shirts, and hems of dresses, weren't too bad, and they could well have been the results of my laundering anyway. But sock-darning I drew the line at; I had always resolutely refused to do it for my own family, and certainly didn't intend doing it for someone who could well afford to replace the odd silk sock.

Then one day, when I was lethargically cleaning Mrs X's bathroom, I noticed that the washbasin was full of knickers and tights; I took it they were there to soak, prior to her washing them through, and after a token swipe at the taps with the cloth I ignored them. They were still there, scummy and grey, the next morning. Heavens, I thought, you'd think she'd have done them by now; if she's not quick about it, the colours will run. A couple of hours later she called me up from my afternoon rest, which I was spending sprawled on the floor playing ball with Cat. 'Do you see those

undergarments?' she said icily, pointing at the washbasin. 'May I ask just *when*' – with heavy sarcasm – 'you intend to get them washed?' Me? I thought, she wants me to wash her knickers? And, following my lifelong practice of answering sarcasm as though it had been rendered in a spirit of perfect reason, I told her just when I intended to get them washed. Never.

No one could be more unpleasant than Mrs X when she was thwarted and from then on, it seemed, she became more and more unreasonable – a punishment, I suppose, for being uppity about the knickers. Even greater magic was expected in the culinary field from ever more meagre rations, and the sheets had to be changed several times a week instead of once. Not that that was a bad idea, taking into consideration the activities of the Mob; but it made for an awful lot of washing and ironing. Finally she came up with the real clincher. If I wished to remain in her employ, she announced, she was afraid Cat would have to go. Cat's presence, and the sight of her sitting in the window, was upsetting the Mob and affecting their nerves. Get rid of Cat? My boon companion, confidante, comforter and blight of my life? Not on your nelly, and certainly not to save the sanity of a band of hairy delinquents and a job which daily became more fraught. I handed in my notice, on the turn. To my surprise, she was quite upset; I really don't think she understood how much Cat meant to me, which was odd when you think how much the Mob meant to her. I worked my month out in an atmosphere of armed neutrality, and then once more packed my bags, my books and my moggie and wandered forth into the wide world.

Mayfair Lady

Standing on the Mayfair doorstep, I gazed up at the tall narrow house and calculated rather fearfully just how many stairs there would be from attics to cellar. Later I was to find to my dismay that there were ninety-eight; after a few weeks of running up and down them umpteen times a day, my thighs would have been the envy of Daley Thompson. This job was another where it was claimed that the employer only visited London occasionally – but this time it turned out to be true, and I don't think I've ever enjoyed myself so much. Sir was immensely rich in a quiet, unobtrusive way, he was considerate, friendly, pleasant – in short, he was bliss to work for. When he was away, which was most of the time, he insisted that I should regard the house as my own; when he was at home, he was so sated with business lunches and official banquets that he asked nothing more than poached eggs on toast in front of the telly. Perhaps as an antidote to his high-powered business activities, he was an avid fan of Coronation Street and we spent many an enthralling hour discussing the carryings-on of Elsie Tanner and the denizens of the Rover's Return. Being right in the centre of London was heavenly; the local corner grocer's was Fortnum and Mason's, and Shepherd Market was fascinating both for its shops and its inhabitants. I used to go for a morning coffee there, sitting in the cafés listening to the ladies of the night discussing their customers. At this hour of the morning they were still a little dishevelled, looking like any other local housewife or typist; but by lunchtime they were absolutely stunning, newly coiffed, dressed and made-up to the nines, putting the other female shoppers in the shade. They could whisk a bowler-hatted, umbrella-ed businessman off the street in a twinkling, without any fuss and have him back out on the pavement almost as quickly, looking much better for his post-luncheon therapy. The local window-cleaner was a mine of information about them; he had the most outrageous stories to tell, of being bundled hastily into cupboards when the lady whose windows he was cleaning suddenly returned home with a customer, and of being offered payment in kind, in advance, for anything from that morning's window cleaning to several months' work depending on the kind of kind.

Taking Sir at his word, while he was away my social life was terrific; I gave what I fondly hoped were elegant little dinner parties in the beautiful Georgian dining room, after which my guests and I would climb the stairs to the equally lovely drawing room for the rest of the evening. My official quarters were right up at the top of the house – a sitting room, bedroom and bathroom with dormer windows looking out across the rooftops of Mayfair. There was access to the roof, too, and on sunny days I nipped up there and sunbathed in the traffic-polluted air, coming back into the house with black specks stuck all over my sun-tan oil. Cat was able to have the run of the roof too and wrought havoc among the pigeons. I was terrified that one of her hunting leaps would carry her over the parapet but she managed beautifully, teetering on the brink of the awful drop as if she were simply climbing a tree. When Sir was in residence, of course, I used my own rooms, pounding up and down all ninety-eight stairs from the kitchen to my bedroom with a pause on the third floor to catch my breath and give my shaking knees a chance to recover. It was a tremendous way to get fit, though; before I finally left I could run up the whole lot without getting even slightly out of breath. But the flight from the kitchen to the dining room was a bind. Sir did give very occasional dinner parties and there was no dumb-waiter, so it meant my ascending and descending at least ten times during the meal, with disastrous results on one occasion when I tripped on my way up and flung a vast bowl of crême brulée, ditto one of peaches in brandy and half a pint of double cream all over the best Chinese silk carpet. Even as I gazed at the resulting mess in horror, I had time to wonder at how far crême brulée could spread; the stairs and half the wall looked like an explosion in a paint factory. All was not quite lost, though – I managed to retrieve most of the peaches and after I'd rinsed the cat hairs and fluff off and doused them with neat brandy they looked quite acceptable and certainly no one complained.

There was only one fly in the ointment. This was the next-door housekeeper, a startling lady of extreme social pretensions and a penchant for the bottle. She never lost the opportunity of telling me how she had come down in the world, driven to the degradation of domestic service by cruel circumstance; but I suspected that her weakness for the electric soup had quite a lot to do with it. This little frailty might have forged a sisterly link between us – I am not averse to the odd spot of conviviality – but unfortunately the poor woman suffered from the most dreadful halitosis. She would emerge from her kitchen door, which was adjacent to mine in the basement area, and by sheer force of breath pin me to the wall at ten paces. Then she would sit at my kitchen table, as I stood at the far side, kneading bread and wishing desperately that I was chopping garlic or making curry, and talk at me while I breathed shallowly through my mouth, the houseplants shrivelled and the paint peeled slowly from the walls. It got so bad that when I heard the click of her door, I would dart smartly into the tiny pantry and stand cramped between the preserved ginger and the coffee beans, hoping against hope that she would give up knocking and go away. Sometimes she went on for so long that I began to fear that she would lose patience and simply breathe on the lock and melt her way in . . . Certainly she was very lonely, and I felt mean and uncharitable at avoiding her so much, but she wasn't the type to whom you could drop a subtle hint although I did, *in extremis*, consider slipping a packet of Double Amplex in with her Christmas card. Gradually she became even more persistent, watching to see when I went in and out and then hammering on the back and front doors alternately until I was forced to answer. And then quite suddenly she disappeared. She had been caught helping herself to her Sir's whisky, and lost her job. After she'd gone, I felt very guilty; I really should have been kinder and more tolerant. I hope she found another job. She'd have made a superb spot-welder.

Sir had been married, but was long divorced and was at that interesting age – old enough to be appreciative of women and young enough to do something about it. Certainly he was never short of female companionship, but not for him the young ladies favoured by the sons of the Middle East. His taste in women, as in everything, was excellent and his ladies tended to be both well-groomed and well-bred. Sometimes they stayed the night, but on their departure there was no sign, apart from both sides of the bed being rumpled, that they had been there at all – no hairs in the washbasin, discarded garments scattered around or empty champagne bottles under the bed. They were not in the least bit patronising towards me but were always pleasant and polite, which was a nice change but had the corollary of no tips. No doubt they felt tipping was degrading, and so in theory did I, but I could never bring myself to refuse one, especially if I felt I deserved it. (And I always did.)

From time to time Sir liked to bestow small gifts on his lady friends, and then the jeweller would be summoned to the house with a selection of the most gorgeous necklaces, bracelets and earrings. I thought this was a marvellous idea, the epitome of what being rich was all about, and looked forward to his visits like mad. There was something satisfyingly incongruous in pawing over a king's ransom in gems in my working outfit of voluminous overall, cotton gloves and tatty slippers; a tiara lent a certain class to even that, somewhat in the manner of Little Madam's diamonds and sacking. The jeweller was a chatty soul once you penetrated the frock-coated façade, and would regale me with society scandal as to which lord had paid off which 'lady', and with what, and how much money some noble duke had spent in his pursuit of happiness. Gazing down at my Brasso-daubed fingers, glittering with borrowed diamonds, emeralds and platinum beyond the dreams of avarice, I reflected that I was in quite the wrong business. Oh to have been a courtesan, rewarded for my favours with the odd ruby or sapphire; but too late now, I'd just have to go on being content with the occasional wild night out at the local pub, followed by a Chinese take-away. Probably fair enough return for the kind of favours I bestowed, anyway . . .

Although I couldn't manage anything in the way of jewels, there *were* certain perks to the job. Quite often the back door bell would ring and there, resplendent in uniform, would be a chauffeur bearing a brace of pheasant or partridge, the victims of a neighbour's shotgun. There was no freezer, so if Sir was away – as he frequently was – there was nothing for it but to eat the game myself. (One or two of the chauffeurs weren't averse to a bit of the wild stuff themselves, and had to be handled with tact and diplomacy.) If Sir was due back shortly, of course, I would simply hang the game; but after the first time that I tried to keep them too long and they had fallen, rotting, from their hook outside the pantry window with a horrid deliquescent plop, I realised that it was wiser (and more sanitary) to eat them fairly promptly. What with game and the odd basket of exotic fruit that arrived in Sir's absence, I gave some lovely dinner parties; it was quite a wrench, after I left, going back to the old familiar spag. bol. and apple crumble and quite a few of my regular Mayfair guests faded from my social circle, the rotten lot.

After I had been working there for about eighteen months, and had got beautifully acclimatised to a life of comparative luxury, the bubble burst. Sir, being a goodly age and as rich as Croesus, decided that the rat race of business was no longer for him, and opted for retirement – in Switzerland. I was so sorry, not only for the loss of a good job but because he was so nice, and even sorrier that he already had a fully staffed home outside Lucerne. No chance of my spending my declining years stuffing myself with Swiss chocolate and learning how to yodel; his Swiss housekeeper had been with him for twenty years. He was very kind, and sorry that my time with him was over; he asked me to stay on in the house until his affairs in London were settled, and it was a temptation. But it could have taken months, even years, and somehow the nagging Puritan work ethic which I tried so hard to suppress kept surfacing and making me feel guilty at living in the lap of comfort, drawing a wage and doing practically nothing. Mind you, I struggled against it and succeeded in stifling my conscience for a couple of months; but in the end I knew that if I didn't get back into the real world, the world of shopping and cooking and cleaning other people's rings off the bath, I'd never want to do it again. I would end up feeling that the world owed me a living, or, like the next-door lady with the inflammable breath, that I had come down in the world; so I gave in my notice, and left. It had been a lovely time.

Private Lives

During my time on Easy Street in Mayfair, I had filled in the long periods when Sir was away by doing the odd spot of outside catering. The agency was only too pleased to have someone they could call on in hours of sudden need or desperate deprivation, such as a City gent finding himself lumbered with providing a cosy meal for visiting businessmen or Cook inconsiderately going down with the flu just before a dinner party. I learned to cook in all sorts of places and with all sorts of equipment though after I'd had to produce a four-course meal for eight with only two saucepans and an egg poacher I learned to take my own pans along with me too. I cooked as much of the menu as possible in Sir's kitchen, and then transported it to that day's customers by whatever means there were at hand. Many's the time I hailed a cab and piled in with my clanking collection of sieves, colanders and whisks, a pan brimful of

soup clutched to my chest as the driver hurtled round Marble Arch on two wheels. He might have driven more slowly had he realised that the backseat of his car was in danger of being swamped by a gallon of madrilene or a casserole of beef bourguignonne. Once I travelled all the way to Kew balancing a whole poached salmon, complete with garnish, on my knee on its salver – not the most comfortable of rides, particularly as the aspic glaze hadn't set very well and slices of cucumber kept slithering drunkenly over the salmon's one visible eye, giving him the appearance of being not only poached but positively stewed.

My favourite client was the young wife of a self-made millionaire in Hampstead; she was years younger than he, being about twenty-two to his sixty, and had replaced the elderly wife who had worked alongside him during the time he was clawing his way to the top. Doubtless the new one fitted his successful image better. She was certainly very pretty – the archetypal old man's darling: she visited the hairdresser every day just to have her auburn hair combed out; her clothes were magnificent, as were her jewels. He was potty about her and spoiled her tremendously, but despite this, she was extremely likeable. She had a great sense of humour and was I think genuinely fond of her old husband as well as of the material comforts he lavished on her. Certainly she was always very affectionate towards him and kept what I assume was her part of the bargain by being an enthusiastic and glamorous hostess on his behalf. She could not, however, cook – and had no intention of learning. I would draw up menus which she would peruse solemnly, her exquisite brows furrowed in concentration, for all of a minute before saying 'Whatever you do will be absolutely fine, Ann – I'll leave it to you.' This suited me down to the ground – I was able to go in for all sorts of flights of culinary fancy which my previous employers wouldn't have appreciated at all. I loved going to the big house in Hampstead where there was no need to take my pots and pans along, as the ultra-modern kitchen was equipped like a picture out of *Homes and Gardens* and could even boast such esoteric delights as a micro-wave oven (very rare in those days), a cherry-stoner, an electric orange-squeezer and an extremely complex food-processor which took so long to put together, take apart again and wash that it was quicker and less trouble to stick to the faithful old Sabatier knife with its blade worn down to a sliver.

Young Wife had recently produced a son – the crowning achievement of Old Husband's life. Previously he had been childless and as far as he was concerned Young Wife could do no wrong from now on. The child was referred to as My Son, with audible capitals, and lived in a suite of rooms with his young nanny and every toy and piece of baby-equipment that Harrods and The White House could provide. He was a good little baby, although very plain. When visitors came to dinner, as they frequently did, he would be dressed in his best and taken downstairs for them to admire; they would peer at him in some embarrassment and grope about desperately for a convincing compliment. He certainly hadn't inherited his mother's looks and I hoped fervently that he had his father's brains. Nanny was a lovely girl, highly trained but not in the least hidebound; she believed in cuddles and picking-up of crying babies, and had none of the starchy sticking-to-the-rules-or-they'll-take-advantage that I had come across in other nannies. Consequently, My Son was a happy baby; and because he was happy, he was good. While I was flinging together the latest dinner in the kitchen, she would hitch him on to her hip and potter happily around me, getting in the way and sticking her finger into the pâté or the mousse for a taste, and scraping out the mixing bowls while she filled me in on the domestic details of life in the house. Old Husband and Young Wife had separate bedrooms with I suppose, visiting rights; once when she took me upstairs for a nosy look-around we discovered all manner of strange devices in a bathroom cupboard, the purpose of some of which baffled even my fertile imagination.

There was nothing as intriguing in the bathroom of my next customer, unless you counted the spare loo-roll cover which was a fearful crocheted purple poodle with sequin eyes.

This victim of my freelance cooking was let in for it by the man who came to paint the Mayfair house (not in oils, just magnolia throughout). He had just finished another job and had learned from the lady of the house that she couldn't find anyone to pop in from time to time and throw together an elegant little dinner; so he asked me if I'd be interested. This sounded just my cup of tea, so I rang the number he had given me and introduced myself. The lady had a breathy baby-girl voice rather like Jackie Onassis at her most cringe-making, and I visualised a fluttery young wife or a helpless-little-me scatter-brained middle-aged one. Which just goes to show

how wrong you can be. I should have known better than to judge anyone by their telephone voice. I had once worked on a switchboard and carried on a torrid flirtation over the wires with a very seductive male voice. It had that dark-brown velvety quality that always makes me go weak at the knees. When we finally met the owner of the sexy voice turned out to be five foot two, with bad breath and a handshake like half a pound of elderly haddock.

The woman on the phone, whilst not as bad as that, certainly didn't resemble the picture conjured up by her voice when I finally met her. To begin with, there was such a lot of it – at least twenty stone and all muscle. Neither was she a wife, and never had been; she was a very successful businesswoman who owned and ran her own factory. Somewhere beneath it all, though, there must have been a tremulously feminine streak, because as well as the teeny-me voice she had the most ultra-feminine house imaginable. It was the sort frequently described by estate agents as 'a bijou residence', and in this case the description fitted perfectly; it was a little jewel of a place, a life-size dolls' house filled with fragile china ornaments, delicate glass baubles that shivered with every breath, pink and white chintz and frills and flounces and silk and satin, embroidered cushions and draped four-poster beds. And two huge, shaggy, Irish wolfhounds called Hengist and Horsa whose waving, yard-long tails made all the precious baubles tinkle and rattle dangerously.

What with them and the Big Business Lady, who could barely get through the smallish doorways, the tiny house seemed crammed to bursting point.

The miniature kitchen was always redolent of the huge chunks of meat boiled for the hounds every day; I never found out what sort it was, but from the smell I think it must have been horse. The only drawback to the dogs, apart from the physical danger of falling over them on the stairs, was the fact that they hardly ever went out; the B.B.L. was far too heavy to walk much, and what they really needed was a good five miles a day. (I volunteered to take them once and they bounded away over Hampstead Heath, completely ignoring my shrieks, and disappeared over the horizon at about 75 miles an hour; it took me ages to get them back and I never risked it again.) Being so confined, they could only use, for their personal needs, the tiny paved and mirrored garden at the rear of the house where they made, through no fault of their own, the most appalling mess which was only cleared away when their mistress could bully one of her factory workforce into doing it. The Augean Stables would have been a bed of roses by comparison; strong men blenched, weaker ones fainted, and I quickly learned to keep not only the kitchen door but all the windows at the rear of the house firmly closed. Between that and the boiling horsemeat, it was almost more than I could stand, and I spent a fortune on air freshening sprays and even considered a surgical mask.

But they were quiet, affectionate creatures, who mooched about like perambulating hearth rugs, watching me cook and resting their heads on the work surfaces while I prepared vegetables. They were so tall that I wondered if it might not be possible to train them to carry trays around on their backs, somewhat in the manner of a howdah on an elephant; it would have been jolly useful at dinner parties. I tried it with Hengist. He was very patient, letting me strap a tray on to him with a belt round his middle, and walking quite

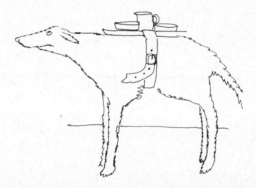

nicely around the kitchen, but then he sat down and the whole kit and caboodle slid gently floorwards. I was glad there wasn't any hot soup in the bowl I was experimenting with. He might not have appreciated half a pint of boiling mulligatawny on the tail, placid creature though he was. So I had to go on serving at dinners in the conventional way, struggling round the table between the backs of the chairs and all the little spindly-legged tables laden with friable objects and holding my breath. It was always a relief to complete the circuit safely and get back into the kitchen, where at least there were only the dogs to tread on.

They were good company and friendly, silent witnesses to those inevitable accidents – the roast dropped on the floor, the cat hairs on the trifle, the fingermarks on the icing – that can all be easily remedied and no one the wiser. 'What the eye doesn't see, the heart doesn't grieve over,' is the favourite motto of every level-headed cook and lest you should think me a slattern, let me tell you that when I worked in a hotel *far* worse things happened – many a diner in the elegant dining room, served by a suave headwaiter, would blench to see the conditions in which his meal was prepared. At least I never had to scoop a cockroach out of the soup, or a fag end from the creamed potatoes . . .

I enjoyed cooking for the B.B.L. Cooking for Mr Y, now, was a different matter all together – as far as décor went, anyway. For one thing, his flat was starkly functional, all chrome, steel and tile; the colours were glaringly primary, with a bright red kitchen guaranteed to have you blinded after ten minutes' working in it and a bathroom completely tiled in brilliant white – floor, walls and ceiling – with not even a plant to relieve the general impression of a public convenience. You could get snow-blindness in there on a sunny day. There was one thing though, it was easy to clean; all you had to do was put on wellies, a mac and a sou'wester and go in and fling buckets of water about a bit. All the chairs in the flat were the kind that are supposed to be scientifically contoured to the body and which in practice are far less comfortable than the overstuffed old club armchair; you couldn't curl up in any of them. Not that Mr Y was the curling sort, or at least not in his chairs. He dressed as severely as his décor – black suit, black ankle-boots, dark tie, pearly white shirt – but he was quite dazzlingly beautiful. All his dinner guests were male, and after I'd served dinner he would send me home in a taxi, having arranged that I'd return in the morning to clean up. The black silk sheets on his bed were frequently wildly disordered, and sometimes there would be a bleary-eyed gentleman staying to breakfast, clad in one of Mr Y's Noel-Cowardish dressing-gowns. They would sit at the breakfast table in the red kitchen while I scraped away at the previous night's saucepans, sipping black coffee and spilling croissant crumbs down their beautiful chests, pulling apart the other guests in a terribly catty way and asking my opinion about them. 'Did you *see* that tie Rodney had on? I *ask* you, with *his* colouring . . .' and 'Giles really will have to go on a diet, my dear – he had *two* helpings of your savarin last night and at *his* age one has to be so *careful* . . .'. It was all great fun and after the last pot had been washed we'd sit in a haze of cigarette smoke round the table and plan the next dinner party menu. Sometimes it would be terribly chi-chi – if he'd asked for larks' tongues in aspic I wouldn't have been at all surprised – and at other times the whim would strike him that it would be 'terribly amusing' to reproduce a school dinner, bangers and mash and spotted dick with lumpy custard. I suppose it reminded them all of the good old days at public school. He was terribly generous, always giving presents to his current favourite, and he once gave me an absolutely adorable pair of scarlet silk panties that were too big for him.

Miss T and her surroundings were a complete contrast to all this trendy sophistication.

·I met her through a mutual friend, a fellow-student of mine. (At the time I was studying for a degree during the few free moments I could find; sometimes I took my textbooks with me on a job and would prop up a book over the stove or the sink, snatching the odd bit of culture as I dashed between the two.) Miss T was another very old lady, but in her younger days she had been not only a very handsome woman but a highly respected academic, an authority on Middle English poetry or early Etruscan shards or something equally esoteric. Now, sadly, her mental powers had waned, and there was only the occasional flash of a previously brilliant mind. I cooked the odd meal for her, but really what she longed for was companionship. She had out-lived most of her contemporaries and was simply waiting out her life in her tiny untidy flat. I acted more as an amanuensis than a domestic – she wrote endless letters to old acquaintances and former students all over the world. She didn't like to dictate because she kept losing the thread, so she wrote it all down in longhand and I deciphered the rambling, sometimes incoherent pages and typed them up into something resembling sense. On her good days she was a stimulating companion, and very helpful to my studies; she could think of lines of enquiry which would never have occurred to me. On the bad days, however, it was an effort for her to concentrate long enough to maintain any sort of conversation at all, and I would read to her from the newspaper while she sat huddled in her rats-nesty armchair.

On those better days she would recount stories of the long hill-walks she used to love, the research expeditions, the many parts of the world she had visited when far-flung travel was not the common thing it is today when anyone with the fare money can get on a plane to the Himalayas or the Gobi Desert or Japan. When she went, she had often been the only Western person, let alone Western woman, within thousands of miles; she had ridden mules over mountains, struggled through dense jungle with bearers to carry her termite-proof trunks, seen glaciers and tundra, and now she was confined to the shabby flat and the only wandering she did was in her mind. The flat, which I did my best to put in some sort of order, was a jumble of souvenirs from her travels; the walls were hung with assegais, Japanese paintings, embroideries from the Hindu Kush, Tibetan prayer-wheels, primitive artefacts. The chairs and sofas were draped and heaped with shawls, rugs, blankets and cushions purchased long before Habitat brought the ethnic look into the world's living rooms; some of them, although shabby with age, were incredibly beautiful and must have been worth a small fortune. I've often wondered what happened to them all when she finally departed on the last long journey of discovery—she had no relatives that I knew of. The colourful conglomeration might very well have been thrown out, unappreciated. Rather like Miss T, they had out-lived their time and place.

By the time she embarked on her final expedition I had moved to another permanent post, but her name caught my eye in *The Times* one day. She had been found seated in her armchair, quite dead. There was a short obituary, briefly mentioning her academic achievements and her travels. I hoped that, having left behind her troublesome body, her spirit was once more tirelessly traversing some beautiful, exciting, sunny upland.

Now that I was out of a job again I toyed with the idea of sticking to this kind of freelance work. There was a lot to be said for it after all: you weren't at the beck and call of the employers' families at all hours of the day and night, you had a sort of semi-professional status which was a comforting boost to the ego and, best of all, when it was over you went away. On the other hand, you had to have a home of your own to work from and enough money to maintain it; you didn't become one of the family, which had been such a nice feature of life at Crumbling Court, and you had to be prepared to cook anything, anywhere, and come up with a meal that was at the very least edible under all sorts of circumstances. No more being forgiven for the fallen soufflé, the watery casserole, the less than perfect meringue. Everything had to be just right or you didn't get the custom again.

And then there was Cat. I couldn't keep hauling her from pillar to post; she was neurotic enough already. No. I needed a home base and couldn't afford one until I had enough customers, so it was Catch 22. Once again, it was time to buy the *Lady*. I would have done better to opt for *The Times*.

Sweet Revenge

Dragging myself out of bed, I staggered to the window and gazed out on to the glorious Cumbrian countryside. Raining. Again. What on earth had possessed me to leave Mayfair and bury myself in the wilds? The advertisement had been so temptingly worded – would I never learn to read between the lines? Still, Cat was enjoying the freedom of the fields after the sooty territory of the London roof-tops. And the scenery was magnificent – when you could see it. Oh well, nothing for it but to leave the hovel which was part of my remuneration – the golden promises made at the interview of renovation and modernisation were perpetually postponed – and trudge along the muddy cart-track under dripping trees to the grotesque neo-classical bungalow where my latest Sir and Madam resided in well-monied comfort. No living-in on this job; it would never do to have the hired help sharing the comforts of central heating, constant hot water and an element-proof roof. In the staff hovel, bracing breezes nipped in through the slates and out through the window frames; there was running water in all rooms (walls, not washbasins) and an exhilarating trek down the weed-infested garden to the al-fresco earth closet. Madam probably conjectured, quite rightly, that the housekeeper would be kept on her toes, rising early and getting to work as soon as possible; even drudgery is more acceptable in warm dry conditions, with access to a flush loo. Madam was in happy ignorance of the fact that, while she was away at her twice-weekly bridge afternoons, her uppity domestic help locked herself into the well-appointed bathroom leading off the main bedroom, and ran a steaming bath, lavish with her employer's Badedas, remaining in a sybaritic world of steam and Imperial Leather until the last possible moment. I only got caught once, when

Sir arrived home unexpectedly; he knocked on the door and demanded to know what I was doing in there. Had Sir resembled Clint Eastwood or Jeremy Irons, I might have invited him in and had jolly Japanese-style mutual ablutions, but unfortunately the only thing Sir was capable of turning on was the tap. Trying to sound as though I was at death's door, I informed him that the heated up leftovers for lunch had disagreed with me, and he, being a confirmed hypochondriac, retreated in panic and took cover in his study. I was surprised not to be issued with a leper's bell when I eventually emerged, with talcum powder applied to my bath-flushed face so that I would look suitably pale and wan.

Once at the house, I let myself into the blissful warmth of the kitchen – once again I was enjoying the benefits of an Aga cooker – and booted the usual spoiled dog out into the garden for its morning constitutional, the results of which the gardener would have to clear up later on. I laid the early morning tea tray, laid the breakfast table, laid the drawing-room fire and, gazing out of the window at the lithe young gardener, suppressed lecherous thought associations. The day had begun. Halfway through the morning, Madam entered the kitchen and said she'd had a wonderful idea. I blenched, having learned through experience that Madam's wonderful ideas always meant extra work for only one person and it wasn't her. I shoved the half-eaten chocolate Bath Oliver, filched from the pantry, into my apron pocket and put on an expression of wary enthusiasm. Wouldn't it be lovely, gushed Madam, if friends came tonight to dinner, drinks, snacks, and brought their visiting son and daughter-in-law? Possibly also their daughter and son-in-law? A lovely big party, such fun. By a massive exertion of willpower I prevented my jaw hitting the floor. Six extra to dinner? Fun? Who was Madam kidding? Fixing a polite smile on my face, I asked what Madam intended serving, as nothing was out of the freezer except four rissoles intended for the evening meal. If I was to clean the silver, polish the furniture, vacuum, clean the bathrooms, arrange the flowers, make a starter, make a pudding and fling round trays of gay little canapés, there would be no time for me to visit the nearby market-town to buy meat. Not to worry, cried Madam, she would go personally and buy a large roast. I was slightly relieved; a roast was easy, I could just bung it in the Aga and leave it pretty well alone, and blame the butcher if it were tough.

Madam took off in a flurry of enthusiasm and the Rolls, taking the spoiled pooch with her, for which I was very grateful. The pooch, despite being disgracefully overfed, spent most of its time underfoot in the kitchen, begging scraps and thrusting its cold nose into unmentionable places when least expected. With them both out of the way, I went into my notorious impersonation of a whirlwind, zooming through the house with the vacuum, dusting, squirting jets of polish into the air in the rooms where I didn't have time to clean. Madam stayed in town for lunch, thank goodness, and I was able to sit for a full hour at the Aga, eating an enormous indigestible sandwich of bacon, baked beans, tomato, cheese and lettuce, all washed down with a can of Sir's beer. I smoked a fag, read Sir's *Times*, sneered at a mistake in the crossword solution and then, burping contentedly, sallied forth into the garden to organise flowers for the table.

The sight of the lithe young gardener, stripped to the waist, as usual brought a sparkle to the eye and a spring to the step. Not to mention a flutter to the heart. His conversation was confined to elementary agricultural matters, but he was beautiful to look upon. I considered the possibility of kidnapping him and holding him as a captive sex-object in the hovel; however, the prospect of long winter evenings, all passion spent, conversing in Neanderthal grunts was a bit off-putting. Still, *until* all passion was spent . . . I wrenched my mind, not without an effort, back to chrysanths and dismissed such unworthy thoughts. It wasn't easy, standing there in close proximity to the L.Y.G. in the steamy hothouse, surrounded by sensuous scents, wanton warmth . . . I hastily selected the flowers and returned to the kitchen, wondering if there was time for a quick cold shower before Madam returned. I made do with a hasty splash at the sink and set about arranging the flowers. It was not a strong point of mine; the flowers kept falling out of the vase or leaning at unaesthetic angles; I battered the stems into submission, using up an entire block of Oasis, and wished that Madam was like other Madams and would do the blasted flowers herself.

The evening arrived far too quickly – there was no time today for my usual two-hour afternoon break when I could return 'home' and flop on the bed, regaining strength for the fray – and with it the guests. Having donned my best plain overall and best white pinny (I drew the line at a cap, after all it was the second half of the twentieth century), I took coats, handed pre-dinner drinks and parried the flirtatious middle-aged guests who see domestic staff as fair game. I wasn't able to avoid them completely – while leaning over the coffee table proffering a canapé to the visiting Madam, the visiting Sir, passing by on the other side with his drink, seized the opportunity for a lightning attack and pinched my rear with a skill that betrayed his Italian ancestry. I retrieved the canapé from the visiting Madam's décolletage, apologised for the sudden lurch, and glared at the visiting Sir. I could see my own Madam wondering if her staff was drunk and deciding to check the cooking-sherry bottle at the first opportunity.

I left the room with what little dignity I had left, reached the haven of the kitchen, massaged my rear to restore the circulation and had a quick swig of the cooking sherry. Might as well give Madam the satisfaction of finding the level lowered; she'd check anyway and I could always say I sloshed some into the gravy. I dished up the first course, rang the bell, and when the guests had stampeded into the dining room I rushed into the drawing room to tidy up the glasses, empty ashtrays and cram the tattered remains of the canapés into my mouth before returning to dish up the main course – roast beef, roast spuds, gravy (sherryless), beans, carrots, Yorkshire pud, horseradish sauce, mustard, the lot. Now for a brief respite – the main course always took a nice long time and I could relax and eat up the leftover starter before having a fag and resting

my weary feet. I wondered what the guests were talking about – sometimes fascinating little snippets of gossip came my way which put quite a different light on some of Madam's friends.

I nipped into the adjoining room and eavesdropped in time-honoured fashion via a tumbler inserted between the wall and the ear, just in time to hear Madam, in the duplicitous manner of the woman in the chicken-pie advert, brazenly accepting a paeon of praise regarding the crisp, golden roast spuds. Madam modestly accepted responsibility for this culinary delight and then heaped insult on injury by claiming she had actually *cooked* them. My blood boiling, I pressed my ear even harder against the tumbler in an effort to discover whether she was going to lay claim to having peeled them, too; to my certain knowledge, Madam had rarely even *seen* a spud in its natural state, let alone penetrated the mysteries of cooking them. The secret of the ambrosial roast spuds is an ancient family secret, passed down by dying mothers to their eldest daughters in an unbroken line of tradition since the days of Sir Walter Raleigh.

Seething at Madam's perfidy, I returned the tumbler to the cupboard and myself to the stove, planning sweet revenge. The profiteroles destined for dessert were already piled glamorously on their dish, the failures artfully concealed within and the partial successes turned best-side-out on the surface. The chocolate sauce steamed gently in the *bain-marie*. On taking up the whisk to stir it, my eye was caught by a gigantic daddy-long-legs, borne through the kitchen window on the gentle evening breeze, straight towards the stove.

In a moment of inspired savagery, I lashed out with the whisk and, with the precision of a Navratilova, volleyed the poor insect to instant death in the molten chocolate lava. Indignation lending strength to my arm, I beat the creature into the sauce until it was only just detectable to the enlightened eye. Later, back at my listening post, I experienced intense satisfaction as I heard Madam ask for the sauce to be passed to her for a second helping. The daddy-long-legs had not died in vain – if there was any justice in the world he had gone direct to insect heaven and doubtless been accorded golden wings and a martyr's crown, his immolation guaranteeing the highest possible rank.

The guests removed to the drawing room and I served coffee, mints, handed round fags and received one or two compliments on the dinner. Repressing the urge to betray Madam in connection with the roast spuds, I demurred modestly and cast a longing glance at the liqueur bottle. I was not offered a drink. It was a pity the men hadn't stayed at the table with the port – there was always a chance of dregs left in the bottle when they did. I left the guests replete, relaxed and slightly intoxicated, and wished I was in the same state. I surveyed the ghastly pile of washing-up in the sink and was filled with an intense desire to leave it and trudge back to my quarters to collapse with a large whisky and Cat. Then I visualised arriving in the cold light of dawn to find the disgusting dishes still waiting, complete with congealed gravy, ossified carrots and solidified choco-long-legs sauce. It was too awful to contemplate; the only thing to do was to gird up my weary loins and wash up now. I drooped at the sink, legs like lead, feet like red-hot knives, varicose veins surging powerfully, and got started. When I got to the pudding dishes, I took a cautious taste of the sauce; it was delicious, subtle, I had obviously made a momentous discovery, a nouvelle cuisine of my very own. My mind wandered dazedly over the limitless possibilities – riz de veau aux ants, soufflé de slugs, beetle beignets, fleas flamande. It could solve the world food crisis – caterpillar concentrate, hi-calorie cockroach compound . . . I could see myself hailed as the saviour of starving millions, a cross between Schweitzer and Escoffier. I determined to write to Robert Carrier directly and offer him my secret sauce in return for a pension sufficient to release me from the bonds of domestic servitude.

Eventually I had finished the millionth pot, given a half-hearted swipe to the work surfaces and peeled the suffocating gloves from my sodden hands. I staggered back down the cart-track, and fell into bed with a large whisky, too tired to read, write, or even clean my teeth. As my eyelids fell like lead, I caught a blurry glimpse of the alarm clock sitting malevolently on the bedside table – 1.30 a.m. Five hours' sleep if I was lucky. My legs throbbed. Also my head and feet. I heaved a huge sigh and went out like a light, and dreamed I had won the Nobel Prize for services to the starving.

My sojourn with this Sir and Madam lasted for about eighteen months, not because I was happy there – I wasn't, particularly – but because the thought of moving again was too awful to contemplate and besides, Cat liked it. (She had open fields to hunt in, and I rediscovered the joys of having a disembowelled shrew dropped in the eye in the wee small hours.) Eventually, however, it had to be faced. The crunch came when, after having given up my day off for three weeks in succession because of their social plans – ever since that dinner party they had been entertaining like mad – I was expected to do so yet again. I objected, and suggested that luncheon and dinner parties might be planned on other days than Wednesday, my supposed free day. Sir went red in the face and mounted his high horse instantly. It was a steed which didn't really suit him; he tended to splutter a lot and little drops of spit would catch in his moustache. This made it difficult to keep a straight face and I was immediately accused of insolence, ingratitude, levity, insubordination and much besides. Instead of giving me a chance to reply he blustered on about he who paid the piper called the tune, falling standards of service, the insidious influence of socialist thought on the proletariat, etc., ending with a diatribe on the subject of the change in the attitude of the domestic class since his own young days. As I knew perfectly well, his father had been in the haulage business in a small way – horse and cart round the villages – and the son, to give him his due, had risen by his own efforts to his present state of affluence; but I hardly felt this gave him the right to criticise my desire to have my day off. Stung, I pointed out that his paying me a wage didn't entitle him to *all* my time – it wouldn't have been so bad if I'd been offered time off in lieu, but I never was. This drove him to even more florid rhetoric; as he paid my wage, and provided a house, I should be prepared, nay, *willing* (he actually *said* nay), to do anything, at any time. Finding his style infectious, I enquired facetiously whether, should he order me to clamber up a gum tree at midnight, I would be expected to do so? *Certainly*, he said. This was so preposterous that I burst out laughing. At this he became purple with rage and before he actually had an apoplectic fit I made my exit, reeling away down the drive still in tucks of laughter. After that I knew I couldn't stay. So I didn't – I left within the week, before he could put his theories into practice. I never could stand heights.

The Merry Widower
and the Passing of Cat

I had been pressing the door bell to no avail for several minutes before it struck me that I couldn't hear any ringing. Must be a broken wire somewhere, I thought, which turned out to be the understatement of the century; *somewhere*? They were *everywhere*. But that discovery came later. At the time I simply resorted to knocking, politely at first and then louder and louder until my knuckles, ravaged as they were by washing-up water and chilblains, hurt too much to continue. Perhaps the man I'd come to see was out. Or he might be ill – my habitually fevered imagination pictured him lying moribund on the floor somewhere, his life slowly ebbing away . . . Perhaps I should go round to the back of the square Georgian villa and peer through a window or two, just in case I might be in time to do some dramatic life-saving. Even if I didn't spot a body it was a good excuse for getting some idea of the kind of establishment it was. The Cumbrian experience had taught me to look before I leapt.

So, after a peep through the letterbox to make sure there was no corpse in the dim hall, I padded round the side of the house, mentally reviewing my kiss-of-life technique and also trying to look as if I knew where I was going, just in case anyone was watching and thought I was casing the joint. The garden was lovely – not a weed in sight, masses of flowering shrubs and a honeysuckle heavy with blossom clambering up the side wall. Definitely a place where it would be a pleasure to work, I decided. The advertisement in the *Telegraph* had given only the barest essentials; 'Widower seeks cook-housekeeper,' it had run, 'live-in, no rough, good wage, start immediately.' Basic to the point of terseness, but it nonetheless contained three elements which instantly attracted my attention, 'Widower' being the first.

'Widower' meant, at the very least, no Madam; and Sirs were so much less troublesome on the whole, being far less prone to instructing their grandmothers in the art of egg-sucking. And of course he might, just *might*, turn out to be short, dark and handsome – I have a weakness for small men, they bring out the mother in me – eligible, comfortably off and with a penchant for middle-aged ladies with hennaed hair, a cat and a burning desire to live in unashamed luxury. Pigs might also fly, but one must think positively, I decided, scanning the skies for any sign of airborne porkers.

The second inducement was 'good wages'. Since leaving my Cumbrian couple, money had been in even more than usually short supply, and it had got to the point where I was having to buy the cheapest food possible not only for myself but for Cat. Faced with a saucerful of odiferous pink gunge, Cat had turned on me such a

withering look of reproach before stalking away to fast unto death if necessary that my heart had been smitten within me. So low were our finances that Cat's despised Moggynosh might well find its way on to my own menu; tarted up with a few spices and then swallowed very fast without breathing, it would be at least stave off the worst of the hunger pangs. The trouble with Cat was that she had become disgracefully gastronomically sophisticated in the last couple of years; anything less than best steak mince or fresh halibut and she would shudder delicately, turn on all four heels and retire in dignified distaste, her retreating backside more eloquent than words. So, 'good wage' was a great incentive, which was reinforced by the third element – 'start immediately'. I was prepared to start yesterday, if necessary; my bags were packed in constant readiness. Once in work, Cat and I would at least be sheltered and fed. There's nothing like penury for rendering the priorities of life crystal clear.

So here I was, clean, bright and not even slightly oiled, all anxious to be interviewed and no interviewer in sight. I pressed my nose against the kitchen window and was relieved to see that the floor was free of bodies, prone or otherwise. The kitchen didn't have a lot else to commend it; an old-fashioned stone sink, a gas stove, open shelves and lino on the floor. Hardly your Sunday-colour-supplement spread, but who was I to complain – a job was a job. The sink was full of dirty pots; presumably the widower operated on the principle of only washing up when there was no clean crockery left, or maybe the 'rough' lady dealt with it from time to time. The widower was obviously a sensible fellow, not given to foolish excesses of hygiene. I was pressing my face against the glass

in an attempt to see round the corner when a voice spoke behind me. 'Having a quick shufti, eh, eh?' it said, and, unpeeling my cheek from the glass, I turned in some embarrassment to see the dearest old gentleman standing there. He looked just like a child's idea of the perfect grandpa; a fringe of white hair surrounding a shiny pink bald pate, a pink face to match, a lovely bristly white moustache and pale blue twinkly eyes – especially twinkly at the moment, having caught me in the act of having a thoroughly nosy peep through his kitchen window. He was wearing old corduroys, a khaki sweater with holes in both elbows and trodden-down bedroom slippers, and he held a trowel in one hand and a pipe in the other.

I loved him at first sight, and the phantom of the dark eligible henna-buff vanished into thin air. Within two minutes we were in the kitchen making tea and chattering as if we'd known each other for ever; any pretence at an interview vanished. We both just took it for granted that I was coming to look after him. He rinsed a couple of cups under the tap – there was only one, no running hot water, I noted – while I brewed up, hunting along the shelves for the tea and finally running it to earth in a tin marked 'Cocoa'. Carrying our saucerless cups, he took me through to the drawing room. 'Do sit down, sit down, my dear,' he invited, courteously sweeping a fortnight's issues of *The Times*, a sock and half a desiccated cheese sandwich off the sofa to make room. I did so, and found myself continuing to travel floorwards until my knees settled cosily around my ears.

I thought back to Little Madam's faded furnishings – these were not only faded but falling apart, at the seams and everywhere else too. The Merry Widower simply didn't see the ravages of time; for one thing he was, blessedly, extremely shortsighted, and for another he had lived with the furnishings for so long that the dilapidations had crept up on him unnoticed, evolving over the years in the manner of a glacier. The curtains were literally hanging in shreds – strips were inclined to come away in your hand when you drew them – but he drew my attention to their beautiful colour, adding that they had been a wedding present fifty years ago. To him, the house was still the lovely home it had been when he first moved into it with his young bride and his inherited patrimony; both the wife and the money were long gone, but he only missed his wife. He had muddled along by himself, eating out of tins and packets and rinsing his socks in the bath, until his son, worried about his health and safety, had insisted that a housekeeper be hired. And I was it; he took me at face value – as I said, he was extremely short-sighted – and I moved in that afternoon, together with Cat. We were in business again.

The Merry Widower certainly did need someone to look after him; the house was one enormous boobytrap and how he'd managed to avoid some ghastly accident was a miracle. All the wiring was so brittle with age that it was positively lethal. As if that wasn't bad enough, he insisted on keeping an ornate museum-piece of an electric heater in the bathroom and several times nearly electrocuted himself, clutching at it for support as he stepped out of the deep old bath with its clawed feet and pitted enamel. Light bulbs exploded regularly and once when I was changing one the whole thing, shade and all, came away in my hand as the flex just crumbled into dust. I don't think he really understood electricity, because he would take the most hair-raising risks. For instance, he would plug about ten different appliances into the one outlet, constructing a complicated jigsaw of adaptors and extensions, and be astonished when he plunged the entire house into darkness, which he did regularly. Then he would toddle out into the kitchen where I was cooking, resignedly, by the light of the gas rings, exclaiming 'I've done it again, haven't I? Done it again? Never mind, soon have it fixed,' and go off to repair the fuses with the heaviest-gauge wire he could lay his hands on. How the place didn't go up in flames I don't know; it was a safety-officer's nightmare. Perhaps the gods were as fond of him as I was. Fatalistically I stored candles and matches in every room and got adept at fishing little bits of wax out of the food when the candle dripped as I was inspecting the contents of a saucepan. If the food was very hot, of course, the wax simply got stirred in and was probably quite beneficial to the bowels.

The 'rough' was attended to by Daisy, who came for the day every Thursday and had done so since the year dot. She was a tall, rangy woman with big red washerwoman's hands and a cigarette permanently attached to her lower lip. She breathed, talked and apparently ate and drank around this fixture, which never seemed to be either a fresh fag or a dog end; it stayed the same length all the time. She was one of those infuriating people who are sure that no one else can do anything as well as they can themselves; it annoyed me at first until I learned to turn it to my own advantage. She would begin to scrub the sink with savage fervour, and when I pointed out that I'd just spent ten nail-breaking minutes cleaning it she would say 'I'll just give it a quick going-over, love, just so it's properly clean', and would doggedly continue, going on to re-wash the cups and saucers which I had just dried. After a while, of course, I simply let her get on with it and didn't bother to do the job in the first place; it was time and effort wasted, and it kept her happy. She was absolutely convinced that no one could cook, clean, iron, wash or shop like she could; or do anything else you could think of, either. You could be discussing something you would have thought completely out of her range, a film or a play for instance, and she would drag on her fag and, squinting through the smoke, say 'Of course, people always told me I should have gone on the stage, I had the gift for it you know; but I couldn't be bothered.' After reading a report in the paper on some model or other, she imparted the knowledge that 'I've always been lucky with my legs, you know;

good legs run in our family. We always Keep Our Legs', and pulled up her skirt so that I could have the treat of a peep at the fabled pins. She had the right number and her knees were in the right place; but Marlene Dietrich she wasn't. She was calmly and unshakeably confident that her looks, and her accomplishments, were second to none; which was very nice for her and frequently amusing for everyone else. We were watching Mrs Thatcher on the television one afternoon over our cuppas. Now surely, I thought, Mrs T is too formidable a lady for our Daise to compete with; even she will have to admit she's met her match here. But not a bit of it; 'What that woman wants is a bit of advice from me,' Daise pronounced firmly. 'I'd soon show her how to put this country to rights'. And she probably would have, too. She could have done absolutely anything and the only reason she didn't was because she 'couldn't be bothered'. For all her irritating ways, she was a well-meaning soul; she really did want you to benefit from the benison of her talents, as long as you appreciated how lucky you were. (After all, as she frequently reminded me, she'd only stayed on with the Merry Widower for so long out of her overwhelming loyalty in the face of tremendously tempting offers to spend her Thursdays elsewhere; one had visions of equerries on their bended knee, mad to secure her services for Buck House.)

The Merry Widower was not a social man; he loved his garden and his crosswords, but rarely had company in. The high spots of his life were his odd visits to London, where he attended occasional regimental dinners and reunions; these affairs were eagerly anticipated and he would spend a couple of days getting ready for them. His dinner jacket, green with age and of a curiously old-fashioned cut, would have to be aired and pressed and trimmed round the fraying edges with the nail scissors. The lapels and cuffs sported a lush growth of fringe which had to be very carefully pruned back every time he wore it. He would take all afternoon preparing for his outing, stretching out the excitement and pleasure like a young girl going to a dance. He would shave extra closely, and trim his moustache to a fierce degree of military bristle so that he more than ever resembled a pink and white prawn. Then, his face bedizened with little scraps of bloodstained loo paper, he would present himself in the kitchen for inspection before his taxi arrived. I would brush him down, tuck in any stray bits, trim off newly sprung frayings, ensure that he had a clean hanky and send him on his way like a small boy to a bun fight.

On these occasions he usually stayed the night in town, returning home the next afternoon after a shopping jaunt with his pockets full of unusually expensive goodies from Fortnum's or Harrods Food Hall. He was particularly fond of Bath Chaps, which he called, with a typical lack of euphemism, Pig's Face, and would delve into the depths of his old overcoat to excavate the delicacy, which would be profusely coated with fluff and flakes of tobacco as well as its proper breadcrumbs. I had to scrape off the hairy bits, which Cat would bolt down with great appreciation. (Surprisingly, the Merry Widower was very fond of Cat; I had marked him down as a Dog Man, and indeed he had been so in his palmier days. His study walls were hung with photographs of labradors he had bred, but he wasn't at all anti-cat; he was, after all, a man of some discernment.) In addition to his Pig's Face he adored Stilton, the riper the better, and persisted in buying a whole cheese at a time from Harrods instead of a nice manageable Safeway's portion. This of course reduced very slowly; there's a limit to how much Stilton a man can consume at a sitting, and I was unable to help, having been traumatised in childhood by the sight of my grandfather mopping up the cheesemites with his bread – 'the best part of the cheese'. After a couple of months I was handing round the cheese at dinner with my face averted and breath suspended; it was like being confronted by Jack the Lad's boots all over again. The Stilton's appearance was bootlike too – brown, leathery and waxy, and when it reached this repulsive stage the Merry Widower would chop it up small – he was too much of a gentleman to expect me to do it – and mix the pungent shards with the dregs left after he had decanted his port, which he strained with loving care through an ancient shirt-tail. The resulting amalgam beggared description. God alone knows what it could have tasted like. No wonder he so rarely had dinner guests; only a more than usually foolhardy man would have tackled that concoction. And then, of course, there was the incident when, rather too full of whisky, the Merry Widower lost control while attempting to carve the duck, and it flew across the table, knocking over the wine as it went, and shot under the sideboard whence he retrieved it, covered with dust, and wiped it nonchalantly on his sleeve before returning it to the carving dish and resuming his attack. People notice these things. Word gets around. The men get sorted from the boys, and you find out who your true friends are.

Yes, the Merry Widower was fond of Cat; out of all the people I worked for, he was the only one who truly seemed to understand not only how much, but why, I loved her. Not, of course, that he would openly give way to sentiment. 'Where's that blasted Cat?' he would enquire gruffly, shuffling into the kitchen in his down-trodden slippers, and Cat – usually so undemonstrative – would roll sinuously at his feet, vibrating with purrs, while he rubbed her tummy. The first time he did this I held my breath; her customary reaction to such liberty-taking was a lightning attack in which, faster than the eye could see, she attached herself limpet-like to the offending hand. Getting her off was like removing a nailed-on plaster and usually resulted in extensive scarring and a surprising amount of blood. My forearms usually bore a network of tribal cicatrices of which a Kikuyu would have been proud. She never laid a claw on the Merry Widower, nor tooth – Cat, whose idea of affection was to sink her incisors into the passing ankle and hang on while you, in agony, dragged her around like an incubus; whose way of intimating that she would look favourably on your throwing her ball for her was to rush at you full tilt as you sat all unaware on the sofa and hit you with stiffened front legs with all her considerable weight behind them. With the Merry Widower, her manner was quite different and lacked the appalling energy which she usually displayed. She would go and seek him out in his study and climb on to his knee, kneading his thighs until they reached a satisfactory consistency and then settling down with him for a chummy afternoon snooze. (She never retracted her claws when submitting my thighs to the same process; as a result they resembled pincushions.) In his turn, he was very tolerant of her goings-on in the garden, even the time she went completely bean-crazy and, as if possessed, stripped off every runnerbean, leaving them strewn on the earth like the victims of a massacre. He sat for hours on the garden seat, throwing her ball or her disgusting spitty toy mouse for her to retrieve, which she did for him; when I threw them, she sat and watched me fetch them.

So I was glad that I was working for him when the awful thing happened. It was on a day when he was up in town after another regimental dinner. There was a knock on the front door, and there stood a man saying he'd run over a cat and did I know whose it might be? I realised afterwards that it was considerate of him to even stop, let alone try to find the owner – people stop for dogs, but for cats they just drive on, as if cats don't count. At the time all I could think was please don't let it be Cat. But I knew it was. I didn't want to see what had happened to her, but of course I had to, and I told myself that at least it was quick, she can't have had time to be frightened or in pain, and the man said yes, that's right. Then he said how sorry he was again and went away; and I went back to the breakfast room and sat and looked at the fire and thought about Cat, her huge green eyes and ridiculous whiskers and tubby body now lying mangled under the honeysuckle until I could face burying her.

When the Merry Widower got home, all jolly with his pockets full of pig's face and kippers, he found me still sitting there and I told him Cat had been killed and it was odd, I hadn't cried. I made a pot of tea and we sat by the fire. He took my hand and said gently, 'Come on now – tell me all about that blasted Cat – how long had you had her?' So I told him all about her – how I'd seen her in the cats' home, and in the face of far prettier kittens, taken her home, a tiny little ugly runt with boot-button eyes and bat ears, rather as I always end up with the straggly pot plant or the flagging sapling – because they seem so much more in need of love. Not that Cat had responded with anything like gratitude; in her that would have been completely foreign and she was always, first and foremost, true to her own nature. How I loved her precisely because she was so lacking in outward charm. And she was more than a companion, a comfort, a confidante and a curse; she was a link with a past life, with me through thick and thin, an unchanging element in changing times. Together we had shivered at Crumbling Court, gourmandized at Mr B's, defied The Mob in Little Venice. We had shared a bed, our last rasher of bacon, and once, inadvertently and to our mutual panic, a bubble-bath. She was, without doubt, completely devoid of conscience, and totally self-centred; all she asked was a full saucer, a warm bed and someone to harass. She knew beyond question that the whole world was run exclusively for the convenience and comfort of Cat. I had loved her dearly and would miss her terribly. By the time I had told the Merry Widower all this, my eyes were swollen from crying, my nose was running and I had made a sodden mess of his going-to-dinner hanky, but I felt comforted. He didn't think I was silly, or sentimental, or tell me to pull myself together; he listened and patted my hand and mopped up, and when I had finally subsided into the occasional hiccup he went and fetched us both a very large whisky. We sat there and chatted quietly until the fire died down. It was a wake for Cat.

The Sorrow of Cyril

With Cat now gone to her happy hunting-ground, there was no longer any reason why I shouldn't take temporary jobs. So when my dear Merry Widower no longer needed me – he retired, like Little Madam, to live with his grown-up children – I was free to explore a whole new field of employment. The jobs still had to be living in, of course, but there were plenty of these available. Employers seemed only too happy to find someone prepared to help in an emergency. And I enjoyed it; there was always variety, and you met the most fascinating people. Like Cyril for instance . . .

Displaying my usual manual dexterity, I deftly sliced my thumb to the bone on the caviare tin and hopped up and down bleeding into the best Beluga and cursing silently. Silently, because Cyril was in the butler's pantry and the last thing I needed was for him to see me being more than usually ham-fisted. Cyril was unbearable; he was the bane of my life. In the first place, he'd turned out to be such a terrible let-down.

When I had arrived at the house on yet another temporary placement, the first thing I saw was this absolute dream of a butler waiting on the doorstep. Talk about gorgeous – around fifty, six foot at least, well set-up but sufficiently flat of tum, dark curly hair, aquiline features – a real Mills and Boon figure of male pulchritude. Wey-hey, I thought coarsely to myself, almost falling out of the taxi in my eagerness to get at him – make his acquaintance, I mean – this is your lucky day, my girl. This'll make a bit of a change from Jack the Lad – what a turn up for the books! Even before I'd reached the front door, my fertile imagination, never at a loss for an image, had the two of us sharing intimate little *tête-à-têtes* over the leftovers, with additional side-benefits undreamt of in my cosy suppers with the Middle Eastern butler, delightful though those had been. To my disappointment, the vision of pure delight ignored my eagerly proffered hand. He merely introduced himself curtly and, turning on his heel, led the way into the house leaving me to struggle with my suitcase and assorted bulging plastic bags.

And that set the tone for our relationship. Cyril had buttled for the same employer for twenty years and, rightly, regarded himself as the most important person in the house – after The Boss, that is. The Boss was the star in his firmament, his reason for being, whose wishes were paramount, whose whims were law; and Cyril found it impossible to understand any other attitude towards his demi-god. Particularly mine, which was a blend of casual friendliness and cheerful disrespect. Cyril saw it as all together too matey. It bordered, to his mind, on familiarity, and he lost no opportunity to put me in my place.

In his eyes, temporary cooks were little higher than the dust, and one could see the phrase 'And who do you think you are?' hovering on his lips every time I overstepped what he considered to be the bounds of propriety suitable to my humble position in life. Once he overheard The Boss and me swopping reminiscences about a newly discovered mutual friend and was absolutely horrified – he refused to believe that I could actually know, socially, anyone in the same orbit as my employer and, tight-lipped, practically accused me of fabricating my own acquaintance with the lady. Unfortunately I compounded my sin by appealing to The Boss for confirmation, which was of course forthcoming, and Cyril looked sicker than ever. He thought me an upstart with dangerous socialist notions of equality – but worst of all, I was A Woman. Cyril Didn't Hold with Women. Women were not People. Men were People, and Women were a lesser breed regrettably allowed to remain within the law. Necessary maybe to some, but not to Cyril.

How unnecessary to him I didn't realise at first; I thought his initial coldness and subsequent air of contempt were merely due to his resentment at the intrusion into his establishment of an insufficiently servile stranger. But one morning, as he deigned to take his elevenses (he kept his own bone-china cup and saucer, separate from my mug) at the kitchen table, I looked up suddenly from the sink and caught him gazing intently at his reflection in the

black glass of the oven door. Unaware of my gaze, he moistened his finger and carefully smoothed an eyebrow, making a little moue at himself at the same time. I quickly lowered my eyes and speculated on his gesture. Was it a clue as to why Cyril Didn't Hold with Women? It was.

Over the next few weeks the clues became more and more obvious. He kept the door to his rooms locked at all times; was obsessively clean and tidy, indeed finicky, in his personal habits; would leave the house late at night without saying where he was going and return in the small hours without saying where he had been; and appeared to have no friends whatsoever – or none that he brought to the house. None of this, of course, need have meant anything at all; but one day the next door chauffeur put me straight on Cyril while giving me a lift to collect some dry-cleaning. He asked how I was settling in, and I said everything was fine, and at least I didn't get chased round the kitchen by Cyril. The chauffeur, an earthy lad with Mellors-like ambitions towards the uppercrust lady for whom he chauffed, laughed coarsely and asked if I was feeling the lack of a man around the place – because if so, Cyril certainly wouldn't be of any comfort – his tastes lay in another direction entirely. (Only he didn't put it quite so politely.) Now, if I were looking for a *real* man . . . I hastily denied feeling any such lack in my life and steered the conversation to the safer subject of Arsenal's chances for the Cup.

This confirmation of my suspicions was, if anything, a great relief. It didn't make me like Cyril any the better, neither did it make me like him less; live and let live is my motto, as long as it doesn't frighten the horses. Each of us has his own particular pathway to Paradise, and if Cyril's was strewn with flowers other than the primroses which carpeted my own, it was no concern of mine. No, it was the sheer self-satisfied efficiency of the man that drove me up the wall. He was sickeningly good at all the domestic tasks; he cooked like a genius, he arranged flowers brilliantly, his laundry (he always did his own, by hand) was spotlessly clean, the whites dazzling fit to blind you. He could get stuck stoppers out of decanters, stains out of table-linen, white rings off polished furniture, fires to light with one match. His ironing was a work of art, and demoralisingly speedy; he could have a pile of immaculately pressed shirts stacked a foot high, looking as if they'd just left their wrappings, while I was still struggling to put the ironing board up. Oh God, he was unbearably efficient; and the result was, of course, that every time *I* did anything in his presence it all went wrong. My soufflés sank, my flowers fell out of the vase scattering water on the gleaming tables, my scones were like bricks, my pastry like cardboard, my mayonnaise curdled. And I scorched things, from The Boss's sheets to the damask table napkins. Things I'd been doing effortlessly and successfully for years – well, successfully by my standards – went haywire. And every time, he would give me an insufferably superior look of withering pity, and say nothing. But on the air would hang his unspoken comment – 'What can you expect of A Woman?'

This, not unnaturally, made me absolutely furious with him and even more with myself; why should I mind, why did I let myself get panicked into such a state of tension that I was in a flap before I even started? But I *did* mind – there I'd been, bodging things for years and perfectly happy about it, and suddenly I *minded*. My self-confidence ebbed to a dangerously low level, and with it my ability to do *anything* right. It got to the point where I could hardly serve Rice Krispies without them going snack popple crap.

On the other hand, discovering where Cyril's sexual inclinations lay did do a little for my self-esteem. His lack of response wasn't, after all, due to my complete lack of allure; I was still lovely old me, but I was just the wrong sex. It was small comfort, but comfort nonetheless.

When I'd been there about three months, and was in a particularly demoralised state, I noticed a slight change in Cyril's demeanour. He began to go out at night a great deal more, and once or twice he even made what could have passed as a friendly comment to me. He began to look almost happy, and one day I could have sworn that he was whistling as he polished The Boss's riding boots to an even more coruscating degree of brilliance than usual. He took to wearing Eau Sauvage aftershave, and his dark curls seemed even blacker and glossier than usual. Then, one fateful evening, the soufflé he was casually tossing together as a treat for The Boss went disastrously wrong, leaking out all over the *bain-marie*, and I suddenly recognised the cause of it all. Cyril was in love.

For a few enjoyable weeks things got better and better. Cyril became almost human, unbending sufficiently to initiate me into some of the mysteries of his esoteric calling. He showed me, for instance, how to dry the inside of a decanter from the outside (hold it upside down under the tap and run hot water over the base – the moisture inside evaporates), how to achieve that mirror-like glaze on boots (*real* spit, and polish, plus a soft cloth, endless patience and a good aim). And how to get the little tiny bits of cork out of a newly opened bottle of wine (give the bottle a quick flick, and the cork will – should – fly out together with a miniscule amount of wine; that's the theory, anyway, and that's what happened when Cyril did it. When I tried I ended up with a half empty bottle of wine and an impressive stain on the wallpaper. And the bits of cork were still floating smugly in the bottle.) He even offered to give me shirt-ironing lessons, but I drew the line at that. No point in raising the shirt-owner's standards of service. As someone said, life's too short to stuff a mushroom, or iron the hidden bits. The men in my life have been lucky if they get an ironed shirt-front, never mind about the sleeves and back; if they want their shirts ironed all over, they can jolly well do it themselves, and more power to their elbow.

I began to be sorry that the job was only to last for six months, and I postponed adding the final touches to the wax figurine I had been patiently moulding from burnt-down dining-room candles; after all, Cyril did take a great deal of work off my shoulders with his shoe cleaning, ironing and frequent cooking of The Boss's special delicacies. And while he was being comparatively bearable, who was I to complain? We even shared one or two of those cosy late suppers I had envisaged so vividly; they weren't everything I'd hoped for, of course, but nevertheless they were very enjoyable, especially if Cyril felt in the mood to contribute a bottle of something cheering from the wine cellar. I liked those evenings best; Cyril drank so little that by the time his glass was due for filling up, most of the contents of the bottle had already disappeared.

These suppers usually occurred just before Cyril vanished into the night on one of his mysterious outings, presumably to meet his beloved. He would appear in the kitchen looking fabulous, immaculately suited, snowy white cuffs showing just the right amount below his sleeves, freshly shaven and absolutely reeking of the Eau Sauvage.

I wondered who the lucky boy was. Whoever he was, Cyril was certainly smitten; one Thursday while Cyril was out buying smoked salmon at Harrods (a task he didn't trust me to do satisfactorily), a delivery man brought a small parcel, and I signed for it. The package was from a very exclusive Bond Street jeweller's, and the temptation to have a quick sneaky peek was overwhelming. I wrestled with my conscience for all of thirty seconds, after which it sank without trace and I opened the box to reveal a gold identity bracelet, very heavy, with chunky links and a nameplate which bore, along with an inlaid diamond, the name 'Bobby'. It was very flash, far more ostentatious than

Cyril's own taste in jewellery which ran to discreet tie pins and plain gold cuff links, and it must have cost a fortune. I hastily wrapped it up again and put it aside; I couldn't put it in Cyril's quarters because, as always, the door to these was locked. When he returned, the carefully selected smoked salmon carried reverently in a basket, he picked up the parcel and took it upstairs without a word. When, later in the evening, he passed through the kitchen on his way to his nocturnal rendezvous, I saw he had a package, beautifully gift-wrapped, in his hand. It had a blue bow on top, and he must have been on his way to give it to Bobby. I did hope it was appreciated, because it must have cut badly into Cyril's savings; in one of his increasingly frequent conversational moments, he had confided that he was saving for his retirement, which he proposed to enjoy in Bournemouth – 'such a nice class of person there, you know'.

This reasonably contented state of affairs continued, and I was happy that Cyril was happy. I should have known it was too good to last, but I wish it could have ended differently from the way it did. Cyril had, as usual, gone out at about ten o'clock at night, but this time he had gone so far as to tell me that he was 'going to a club with a friend – I'll be late back, but don't wait up, Mrs W, I've got my key.' So, The Boss being away wheeling and dealing, I had the house to myself, and proposed to have a thoroughly indulgent evening. Accordingly, I took a long and lazy bath, washed my hair, helped myself to a disgustingly large shot of Cyril's whisky – he rarely drank and I was impatient at the level never sinking in the bottle – and settled down cosily in the breakfast room to watch the late-night film. This turned out to be far scarier than I'd anticipated, and watching horror movies alone has always been beyond me. (I am probably the only person in the world to have seen half of *The Beast With Five Fingers* three times; at the same point in each attempted viewing I leap for the off-button, eyes averted from the screen, and then spend the rest of the night convinced I can hear something unspeakable scrabbling across the floor.) After ten minutes' viewing, the hairs on the back of my neck began stirring ominously, after fifteen they sprang smartly to attention, and after fifteen and a half so did I and hastily switched off. Bed, I thought, that's the ticket, with sheets pulled well over the head. I downed the whisky and then, as I crossed the kitchen bedwards, I heard it. A scratching and fumbling at the back door.

It would be inaccurate to say I was frightened; I was petrified. It seemed ages before I was able to move, but at last I nipped back, heart pounding, into the breakfast room and very carefully squinted through the curtains. There was a figure on the back step. The relief was considerable – at least it was some human agency. I wouldn't have to go to bed garlanded in garlic and clanking with crucifixes after all. Tiptoeing to the back door, I shouted bravely 'Go away!' Hardly original, but to the point. 'Can't find the keyhole, 's gone,' came the reply, in a voice that was distinctly slurred but equally distinctly Cyril's. I was shocked – Cyril, sozzled? – something must be wrong. I got the door open as quickly as possible and Cyril practically fell into the kitchen.

He looked dreadful. Gone was the immaculate gentleman's gentleman, and in his place was a grey-faced, red-eyed apparition with dishevelled hair and a darkening bruise on his cheek. His tie was wrenched askew and there was dirt on the knees of his beautiful trousers. Seeing me, he made an immense effort to pull himself together. In reply to my frantic enquiries as to what had happened, he very carefully enunciated "Sall right, 's nothing, fell over, 's all,' and with an even greater effort, very clearly, 'Please don't fuss, I shall be all right. Go to bed, it's very late.' Exhausted by this effort and looking like a man who had been hit by a sledgehammer, he walked with dignity up the stairs, only stumbling once, unlocked his door without too much difficulty, and with a final 'Goo' night' disappeared inside. Gosh, poor Cyril, I thought, he's going to feel like death warmed up in the morning. Must have been some party at that club, they must have been really celebrating. Perhaps, I thought unworthily, he and Bobby have got engaged. He didn't seem very happy, though; but then I expect he feels sick. Probably throw up and feel better soon. I know, I'll make him a cup of tea; the old devil could probably do with one.

So I went down again and made tea, and carried a large mug of it up to Cyril's door. Pausing outside before I knocked, for the second time that night I heard an unaccustomed sound. Pressing my ear against the door, I listened hard, and after a few moments the unbelievable truth hit me; Cyril was weeping, great painful sobs, the awkward tearing sound of someone crying who hadn't cried for years and had forgotten how to do it. It was heart-breaking to hear; I couldn't have gone to my room and left him like that. I tried the door handle. It was unlocked. Still carrying the mug of tea I slipped quietly into the rooms which had, up to now, been sacrosanct. There was a tiny hall with three open doors; on the left, with the light on, a bathroom. On the right, a darkened sitting room. The weeping came from the remaining room.

I tapped on the door and said 'Cyril?', standing there foolishly still clutching the mug of tea. There was a strangled gasp and Cyril's voice, sounding choked and trembly, said 'Yes?' Pushing the door wider, I went in and saw him. He was seated, still in his bedraggled suit, on a stool in front of the dressing-table, staring at his reflection. He sat with feet apart and hands on his knees, and suddenly I could see that he was very nearly an old man. His face was blotchy now, wet with tears, his nose was running and he made no attempt to wipe it; he simply sat and stared at himself in the mirror. On the dressing-table was a bottle of hair dye, a dye-stained toothbrush, and a denture box.

He dragged his eyes away from their own reflection and they met mine as I stood, appalled, behind him. 'He hit me,' he said. 'He laughed, and then he hit me. He knocked me down.' 'Oh Cyril,' I said, and as the tears ran down his face again I couldn't think of anything to do except go and put my arms round him. So I did, and he turned stiffly and buried his head on my midriff, and the awful sobs burst out of him again. It was a good five minutes before the storm was over; by then the whole story had come out and he was leaning against me, all dignity gone, just a very sad, deeply humiliated man whose love had been most cruelly spurned. He had finally declared himself to Bobby, his golden boy, his lovely lad, after weeks of wooing him with lavish presents and expensive meals, and Bobby had laughed in his face, had called him an old fool, had told him in effect that he'd been taken for a ride; and then walked out of the club. Distraught, Cyril had run after him, pleading that he shouldn't leave, that he would still see him; and Bobby had turned and hit him in the face, knocking him to the ground before walking, laughing, away. For a proud and fastidious man like Cyril it was a traumatic experience, and as soon as he was able to stand he had gone, in a state of shock, to a strange bar and drunk as fast as he could to try and blot out the pain. It hadn't worked, and he had staggered home in a daze.

By this time I too had wept, with pity and anger, but eventually it was over. Our unexpected intimacy seemed suddenly to strike Cyril and he sat up, reached for tissues, cleared his throat and tried to regain something of his usual composure. He apologised; I demurred; we were both embarrassed. Then I thought, this is silly, we can't just forget it all, can't just pretend it didn't happen. Things can't be the same.

'Come on,' I said, 'Let's go down to the kitchen and have a cup of tea. Could you manage a bacon sandwich?' He blew his nose, stood up and managed a smile. 'Do you know, Mrs W,' he said, 'I believe I could. But,' he added, 'do make sure that the bacon is sufficiently crisp.' I knew then that he would find the strength to get over the worst of the affair – and that things wouldn't be all that different, after all. I was surprised to find that I was glad.

Crooks and Nannies

'I like gin,' said Crispin hopefully, leaning across the kitchen table and inhaling noisily over the bowl in which I was attempting to make a gin-and-grapefruit sorbet. 'Do you now,' I muttered absently, concentrating on folding the stiffly beaten egg whites smoothly into the mixture. 'Daddy likes gin too,' he went on conversationally. 'Daddy likes gin a *lot*.' You can say that again, I thought, having spent a tricky five minutes the previous night evading the clutches of Daddy who, primed with a surfeit of pre-prandial G and T, had trapped me in the pantry. Out of the mouths of babes and sucklings . . .

'Can I have some?' he went on. 'No,' I said shortly, keeping one eye on the contents of the bowl and squinting with the other at the recipe, propped against the gin bottle. Crispin was silent for a whole blessed peaceful minute, and then 'Shall I scream?' he offered, looking up at me through sinfully long eyelashes to assess his chances. 'Don't bother,' I curtly advised him, 'gin is *not* for little boys.'

He changed his tack. 'I *love* you, Anny,' he crooned, flinging an arm round my neck and pressing a sticky kiss on my cheek. I said 'Oh, Crispin, I'm *busy*,' but I gave him his kiss back before concentrating again on the sorbet. Narked at not retaining my full attention, he played his trump card. 'Want to wee-wee,' he announced triumphantly. That did it; sighing heavily and abandoning the sorbet to its fate, I seized Crispin and set off for the loo at a fast hand-canter.

Crispin was four, affectionate, bright, beautiful and about as house-trained as your average yak. His mother didn't believe in potty-training – or, as far as I could make out, any other sort of training. 'Children are simply little unspoiled souls, simply little animals,' she would declaim, traipsing round the bedroom in one of her voluminous kaftans while I, on my knees, sopped up yet another puddle on the carpet. 'When they're ready to learn, they'll learn – nature is the best teacher. Leave it to nature.' Leave it to nanny, more like, I would reflect bitterly, scrubbing at the spreading stain and wondering if Earth Mother had never seen a mother cat sternly teaching kittens to use a sand-tray.

All very well for her, out on her lecture rounds, delivering talks to groups of less privileged mothers on the importance of a childhood free from what she described as 'the inhibiting impositions of conformity', which would apparently prevent their offspring from attaining their full potential by requiring them to use a potty, eat with cutlery and refrain from spitting at their grandparents. She, unlike the luckless audiences amongst whom she sought to spread her gospel of the child as Noble Savage, had help at home and plenty of it. When Crispin piddled on the Persian rug or Jessica gave the tadpoles a spin in the blender, it was Nanny or Cook who dealt with the resulting stain, smell or Seafood Surprise.

I was 'filling in' as a temporary cook for a month or two while the regular incumbent got her varicose veins fixed. Crispin was with me in the kitchen because it was Nanny's day off, and because it was his favourite place anyway; Jessica, thank the lord, was at school. She was an intrinsically evil eight-year-old, with a morbidly inventive turn of mind, a natural candidate for membership of Charles Addams's Munster family. I had been told several times about how she had dismembered a previous nanny's pet budgerigar and was thankful that when she was at large over the weekend, I was off duty which was one of the better aspects of the job.

Generally, I tried to take jobs where there weren't any children – not because I am a founder member of the Friends of Herod Society, but because they meant extra work and, usually, a nanny to be dealt with too. Some nannies could be distinctly odd; perhaps the rigours of their calling made them that way, or perhaps it was their natural defence against the heartache of leaving the children they came to love, as they eventually had to. The starchy, no-nonsense old-fashioned nanny of legend still survived in small isolated pockets of resistance, but they were a dying breed; the modern ones ranged from highly trained, progressively minded professionals through jolly, jean-clad friends-of-the-family to the ubiquitous foreign au pair who often had no idea at all of how to cope with their charges, or even to communicate with them.

Crispin's present nanny, Claire, came somewhere in between the last two categories. She was a young actress, 'resting' at the moment, easy-going and agreeably slapdash. She let Crispin go to bed when he was tired and eat when he was hungry. Her attitude to him was always warm and affectionate, although sometimes alarmingly casual; she let him do what seemed to me the most horrifyingly dangerous things, and if I remonstrated she would merely say, 'Well, if he falls (or cuts himself, or drowns, or gets eaten by a bear) he won't do it again in a hurry.' Perhaps it was just luck, but her 'method' seemed to work.

Crispin was adventurous but rarely came to any harm. Sometimes, if she'd had a hectic morning of it, perhaps being hassled by Earth Mother who always seemed to descend like a disrupting whirlwind just as Crispin was playing quietly, she would fling into the kitchen, chivvying Crispin before her, and throw herself dramatically into a chair. Lighting a fag and casting her eyes heavenward, she would blow smoke down her nose so that she looked like a war-horse and swear that she couldn't stand it another day. 'God knows why I stay!' she'd wail, flicking ash all over the floor or into whatever I was mixing. 'I could be playing Hedda Gabler, they wanted me to, you know!' The mysterious 'they' were never specified and I didn't like to ask for fear they turned out to be the local amateur dramatic society which consisted of fifteen stage-struck ladies and the vicar. Then, as Crispin grizzled for his lunch, 'Oh, Ann, for heaven's sake give the little horror something to eat — anything'll do ... and while you're at it make a ground-glass sandwich for Old Bossyboots — I'll serve it to her myself with the utmost pleasure . . .' Crispin, placidly ignoring the histrionics, would eat macaroni cheese with his fingers, happy in the certain knowledge that once Claire had got it all off her chest he would be lifted on to her knee for a cuddle and a story.

Crispin wasn't the only member of the family who hungered for a cuddle from Claire — although he was the only one to get it. Poor Nanny was not only pestered by Earth Mother, but by Daddy too; his gin-induced grab for me the previous night was as nothing to his persistent pursuit of Claire. Feeling as she did about E.M. and her constant nagging, she would normally have been only too happy to return tit for tat through the medium of an enjoyable little dalliance with Daddy. Unfortunately he wasn't at all her type, which inclined to darkly intense young men with wild hair and hip measurements in single figures; Daddy was running to fat, with a bay-window front, and short back-and-sides hair which he controlled with Brylcreem. Like a lot of middle-aged men who should know better but rarely do, he fancied his chances with girls young enough to be his daughter. Poor Claire was for ever fighting off his advances, but the more she fought the more it seemed to inflame him. He probably believed in the old male-chauvinist creed, 'If she says No, she means maybe — and if she says maybe, she means Yes', and I think he saw Claire's evasions as maidenly reserve which he prided himself on being able to penetrate eventually. It obviously never struck him that she was motivated by simple distaste.

He lay in wait for her round corners, in the bedroom corridors, in the conservatory, outside the bathroom; anywhere where, unobserved and unsuspected by E.M. who would have flayed him alive, he might have a chance to get his clammy hands on Claire. At first, she'd tried being reasonably polite and good-natured in parrying his advances, but this proved to be worse than useless – he merely took it that she was playing hard to get. 'The conceit of the man!' she groaned to me over our nightcap of Horlicks. 'He sees himself as the answer to a maiden's prayer, probably expects me to be grateful, or else he's got some medieval notion of droit de seigneur. It's not even flattering,' she went on, 'his idea of a subtle pass is to grab my backside when I'm leaning over the bath washing Crispin. Pure men's locker-room stuff – he must have the sexual mentality of a randy fifteen-year-old.' She gloomily topped up her Horlicks with cooking brandy. 'Tell him you've got a boy-friend who plays for the Barbarians,' I suggested. 'Six foot six and eighteen stone, and dead jealous'. 'He's *seen* my boy-friend,' she sighed. So had I. Six foot six, nine stone, wringing wet and into open relationships. 'Oh well,' I said, 'have to think of something else, then.' 'I'll just have to sink to his adolescent level,' Claire decided. 'Next time he starts his hankypanky I'll tell him to push off (only she didn't say push) and keep his wandering hands to himself, and threaten to scream or something.'

But that didn't work either. The man had the hide of a rhino. I thought of Jack the Lad at Crumbling Court; he'd suffered from delusions of irresistibility too, but somehow his enthusiastic overtures hadn't been offensive. They'd been so open, earthy and bucolic – if he wanted to pinch your bottom or promise to 'do you a bit of good', he didn't lie in wait until he got you alone. He just carried on regardless of who was there, and his manly pride was satisfied by a shriek of 'Ooh, you are a one!' He never persisted if it was clear you were neither interested nor amused. But not Crispin's Daddy; he was sneaky, the sort of man who would watch you, and catch you, unawares. So Claire grew ever more annoyed. Of course, it was sexual harassment of the most blatant kind, but this was a few years before you could officially do anything about it; it was just something women had to cope with as a fact of life.

'Perhaps he's only trying it on,' I mused during one of our frequent dodging-Daddy discussions. 'You *could* try turning the tables on him. Next time he starts, come on strong, give him the old heavy-breathing routine and call his bluff.' (I knew it *could* work; a notorious self-styled ladykiller of my acquaintance had been stopped in his tracks at a party by a victim who took his hand, gazed at him langorously through half-closed lids and breathed 'You talk a good game, Big Boy; come on, let's see if you're as good as you think you are!' Within five seconds he had dropped her like a hot potato and was avidly seeking the protection of his wife's side, scared out of his wits and passing the peanuts with the best of them.) Claire considered this idea for a moment. 'I'll give it a try,' she said. 'You never know, it might do the trick. I'll work out a scenario, lay it on really thick. Frighten the life out of the creep, with any luck.' She draped herself over the chairback, lowered her eyelashes and husked 'Come up and see me sometime' just to get in practice.

The following evening I was desultorily wiping down the sink when Claire pelted into the kitchen, distinctly dishevelled and caught between hysterical laughter and real panic. She slammed the door behind her and turned the key before collapsing against the fridge. 'It didn't work!' she gasped. 'Quick, give me a brandy!' I

hastily poured a large medicinal shot and she downed it in one gulp before pouring out the story. Daddy, apparently, had seized the opportunity to run his hand up her leg as he followed her up the stairs, and Claire had put the bluff-calling technique into action. Swinging round to face him, she had summoned up all her dramatic talent. Leaning sexily on the banister, she fluttered her lashes, moistened her lips, breathed stertorously and murmured huskily, 'All right, you win – I can't resist any more, my body cries out for you, I ache for your embrace – take me, I'm yours . . .' and swayed towards him in the manner of a sapling in a high wind. To her horror, instead of shrinking back in dismay, Daddy leapt for her, his face emblazoned with lust – but luckily for her, passion weakened his knees to the extent that he missed the next stair, tripped and fell at her feet, cracking his nose on the step and giving her the chance to leap over his prostrate body and make for the safety of the kitchen. It had been a nasty moment, and I apologised for suggesting the ploy in the first place. That, plus liberal applications of the brandy, was the least I could do.

For the next few days Daddy kept his distance. Perhaps the swollen nose had dampened his ardour. Once it had subsided, however, he resumed his attentions more flagrantly than ever and Claire was getting desperate. 'It's no joke,' she complained. 'I'll have to do something to stop him once and for all. Next time I'm going to tell him that if he doesn't pack it in I'll drop a hint into Earth Mother's shell-like ear, and I mean it.' 'She'd kill him,' I said, 'and sack you.' 'I don't care,' Claire said, 'I've had enough. Much as I love Crispin, I can't see any alternative.' But, in the event, it wasn't Claire who enlightened Earth Mother as to her husband's activities; it was Jessica.

Of course, it all happened over the weekend, when Jessica was at home and I was away – it would do, just my luck. I missed all the fireworks and returned on Monday morning to nothing but the burnt-out sticks. There was no sign of Claire; but propped against the brandy bottle in the recesses of the kitchen cupboard was a letter addressed to me. It was from Claire, and it gave me the whole sordid story.

On the Saturday Earth Mother had a speaking engagement sufficiently far away for her to leave before lunch, which meant that Claire was blessedly free of her for the whole day. It also meant that she wouldn't be returning until mid-morning on Sunday – even better. Of course, there was the fly in the ointment; Jessica would be in Claire's care, as well as Crispin, but one must be grateful for small mercies. While the cat was away the mice could play, and Claire rang her willowy boyfriend Mark, and invited him for the night. Unfortunately, Daddyo decided that the rat could play too – this was what he'd been waiting for, his wife away for the night and Claire, as far as he knew, conveniently alone and accessible. Crispin was packed off to bed uncommonly early, having been cunningly exhausted by a very long tricycle ride to the village and back. Jessica proved more difficult; she demanded to stay up and watch a particularly unsuitable horror film on the television. Claire had to resort to bribery – the promise of the loan of the Marquis de Sade's memoirs – before she eventually dragged off to bed reluctantly and Claire was able to join Mark in the bedroom. By this time it was after eleven, the house was quiet and there was no sign of Daddy; he was at a business dinner – or so he said – and wasn't expected back before midnight. So Claire and the boyfriend, overjoyed at this rare opportunity, busily set about making up for lost time. So busy were they, in fact, that they failed to hear the bedroom door open; the first time they knew they were not alone was when Jessica, after observing the action for several minutes, tapped Mark on the shoulder and announced, 'I know what *you*'re doing, and I shall tell my mummy in the morning you were doing things with Claire. Unless,' she added, with a terrible smile, 'you give me some money.'

Mark, his mind still firmly on other things, was speechless with surprise. Claire, however, wasn't. Clutching the sheet around her, together with what shreds of dignity she could muster, she fought fire with fire and informed Jessica that she too would have something to say to Mummy in the morning. Namely, about sneaky little girls who barged in where they had no right to be and threatened blackmail. 'Pig,' said Jessica succinctly, 'I know who Mummy'll listen to.' With which, plus a hideous grimace, she withdrew and presumably returned to bed. Claire was all for returning to the matter in hand, as it were, but Mark had been put completely off his stroke and they eventually went to sleep, frustrated but not particularly worried by Jessica's parting shot.

They were not, however, to sleep undisturbed. Just after 6 a.m., Claire awoke to see a shadowy but familiarly bulky figure standing by the bed. It was Big Daddy, rising refreshed from his slumbers and come to claim his unconjugals. Before she could yell, he had pulled back the covers and was climbing into bed beside her, whispering 'Ssh!' and clutching at her wildly. Then she did yell – for

one thing, his hands were freezing cold. Mark, sleeping on the other side of her, shot up in bed and, seeing someone else groping his girl, promptly demanded to know What the Hell he was doing. Open relationships, O.K., but he drew the line at troilism. It must have been an astonishing sight – all three in a state of shock, the two men bolt upright with Claire stark naked between them like, as she put it, the ham in a sandwich. Then came the action: Mark leapt for Big Daddy, who fled for the door and, wrenching it open, fell out into the hall with Mark right behind him. They landed in a heap, Mark naked and Daddy in his best seducing gear of black silk pyjamas with gold monogram. Claire, leaping after them, got to the door just in time to see the first punch landed. She also saw the figure of Jessica, crouched on the top step of the stairs, an expression of unholy glee on her face. Seeing Claire, jammed in the doorway, Jessica transferred her gaze from the two struggling men and, with a triumphantly evil grin, went back to bed for the second time that night.

By the time Earth Mother got home, Mark had issued an ultimatum to Claire – she was leaving with him at once, or else it was all over between them. He had also issued one to Daddy; if he ever set eyes on him again, he would beat the living daylights out of him. Mark may have been willowy, but he was surprisingly effective in an emergency. Claire was enormously impressed. Big Daddy had taken himself off somewhere to lick his wounds, nurse his black eye and concoct a story to account for it. His daughter forestalled him. No sooner had Earth Mother crossed the threshold than Jessica, all wide-eyed innocence, was recounting the tale of how, frightened by a nightmare (!), she had sought comfort from Nanny only to see 'Daddy *and* another man coming out of Claire's bedroom, and Claire had no nightie on *nor nothing*'. Earth Mother erupted like Vesuvius. Her theories of unrestricted animal freedom did not, she made it abundantly clear, extend to her husband. In the ensuing maelstrom Claire just had time to pack her bags and write to me before taking off in Mark's old banger of a car. Not, though, without first telling E.M. a few home truths which raised the tantrum level even higher. And not without taking a very fond farewell of Crispin who, remarkably well-balanced child that he was, accepted it all very calmly.

I looked after him for a couple of days until his mother found a new nanny. Her ideals again went by the board; she was taking no more chances. The new nanny was stout, middle-aged, uniformed and of the old school. Within a fortnight she had Crispin toilet-trained, Jessica thoroughly cowed, and an iron routine established which brooked no arguments. Big Daddy wouldn't have stood a chance, even if he fancied moustaches. I never met Claire again, although we wrote for a while; but I did see her, not long ago. She was beautifully gowned, elegantly coiffed, tremendously sophisticated, and she was extolling the merits of some exotic drink in a TV commercial. Remembering our merry evenings over the Horlicks and cooking brandy, it seemed appropriate.

Stirring Times

By the time I had reached the half-landing, my arms were on the point of breaking. If it had been for anyone else, I wouldn't have bothered – but I couldn't disappoint Diana. So I stopped and panted a bit and rested my burden on a convenient chest of drawers. The basin I was carrying was the size of a wash-tub; and it was full of Christmas pudding mixture, and I was taking it upstairs, in constant peril of putting out my eye with the wooden spoon which was stuck into it, so that Diana could have her lucky stir. She certainly needed some luck. It was ten days to Christmas and she had come down with the measles. No fun when you're twenty-nine and even less when you have five children under the age of ten and a big family Christmas looming. So I hoisted the bowl again and staggered the rest of the way to her room.

I'd been called in to help with the emergency; the agency had been in a complete tizwoz, no one was free to work at Christmas time, and Diana's husband Rodney, faced with the chaos of a family house party with his wife out of commission, had begged them to find someone – anyone! – who would be prepared to help. He got me, which was a bit hard on him I suppose, but beggars can't be choosers. Actually I was glad to have somewhere to go; Earth Mother's cook had returned, varicose veinless, and I wasn't exactly wild about the prospect of a lonely Christmas. And anyway as usual I needed the money.

I must admit I blenched a bit when the agency gave me all the details which, wisely, they refrained from doing until they'd ascertained that (a) I was free, and (b) I might be prevailed upon to take the job. Five young children, their father, two sets of elderly grandparents and a couple of teenagers – a niece and a nephew –

whose parents lived abroad, too far away for their children to join them for the short Christmas break from boarding school. And a measly mum. A total of thirteen to be fed and watered for a month. Lucky thirteen, I thought in a positive way, stifling the echo in my mind of the bingo-caller's 'unlucky for some'. I told the agency I'd do it, and then wondered uneasily if my appetite for new experiences had once more led me to bite off more than I could chew.

The harassed young father came to pick me up, together with my luggage, two hours after the agency had contacted me. He was about thirty-three, tall and slim with fair curly hair and anxious grey eyes; very friendly, very polite, and terribly grateful. He kept reassuring me all the way down to his farm in Berkshire that they'd all do their best not to make too much work and were determined to try and help out 'though', he said, with a nervous apologetic laugh, 'I'm afraid my mother and my ma-in-law aren't exactly handy around the house – it's the horses, you see. . . .' Apparently the entire family was mad keen on horses – riding, jumping, showing and breeding – and devoted their time to things equine to the exclusion of such domestic trivia as cooking. I reassured him that as long as they didn't expect Cordon Bleu catering three times a day, for thirteen people, for a month, we'd all manage beautifully. I had my fingers crossed while making this optimistic pronouncement, naturally, not having met the household yet; but if they were anywhere near as nice as Rodney, it shouldn't be too difficult.

By the time we reached the farm, we were getting on like old pals and even before I got there I was beginning to be sorry that it was only a temporary job. As we drew up outside the old red-brick farmhouse, a mixed flock of dogs and children rushed out to meet us – I thought it was three dogs and four children, but in the general mêlée of hugs, licks, barks and cries of 'Daddy!' I couldn't be quite sure. Once he'd reappeared from under their tide of welcome, he took me straight up to meet his wife Diana; she was sitting up in bed looking very pretty, despite the spots, and also looking every day of twenty, with her long red hair in plaits. Within seconds I had recognised a soulmate; she was mad about babies, cooking, cats and horses. I felt like her elder sister. She had been through the usual post-school cookery course attended by girls of her class, I discovered later, and had thought of going in for the fashionable career of directors' lunches or party catering, but had instead met Rodney. They had fa'' ⸻ ⸻ ⸻nd madly in love, married in enormous haste and a haze of orange blossom, and settled on his farm where they equally instantly began producing their brood of children. Her ambition was to have ten, preferably five of each.

Up to now they had produced three girls and two boys, and after settling me down in my pretty bedroom I was taken down to be introduced. The eldest was nine, a girl called Caroline with her father's blond hair; next came Fred, just eight, red-haired and blue-eyed; then Maggie, six and three-quarters, fair curls and grey eyes; then James, four and a half, silky ash-blond hair and blue eyes; and then the baby, Jane, fourteen months, plump, delicious and sunny, with red curls and grey eyes. They were all utterly delightful, quite the nicest children I'd ever encountered; healthily naughty on occasion but never, or at least not during the time I was there, unkind or temperamental or mardy. I also met the gaggle of grandparents; two patrician grandmothers, redolent of county tradition, down to the twinsets and pearls and complexions rendered ruddy with outdoor living and long periods of exercising horses in all weathers; and two huntin', shootin' and fishin' grandfathers, bluff and hearty, ex-military and upright. They all greeted me without the slightest trace of patronage; it was Christian names all round from the start and a sherry or two before lunch every day, brought out to me in the kitchen if I was busy – as I always was. Thanks to Diana's training, the kitchen was modern and well-equipped, labour-saving and with a gorgeous view out over the paddocks; it was heaven to stand doing the washing-up with the sight of brood-mares and their foals in front of me.

The niece and nephew weren't due to arrive until three days after I was installed, so I had a little while to get myself accustomed to cooking for large numbers before the real rush began. They were gratifyingly easy to cook for; with so many children Diana had never had time or inclination to let them develop any faddiness and the entire family had remarkably healthy, unfinicky appetites. They all had breakfast together, which was convenient, and lunch too; but in the evenings I cooked a meal for the children at six o'clock and dinner for the adults for eight, which meant a certain amount of sleight of hand with potatoes, and making two puddings at once. Rodney took trays up to his wife – no running up and down the stairs for me this time around, and I was very grateful.

I did, though, take the Christmas pudding upstairs; all the children had been into the kitchen for their stir of the glutinous mass, so had Rodney and the grandparents, and Diana couldn't be left out. While she was having her stir, the car bearing the niece and

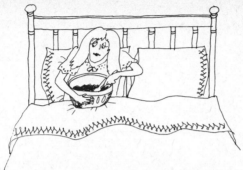

nephew arrived, and once more chaos broke out as a tidal wave of mixed infants and animals engulfed the pair of them. 'Oh goody,' said Diana, peering out of her window, 'there they are. Just in time for their stir,' so I had to stagger down to the kitchen in time for Robert and Sarah to take their turn. It must have been one of the best mixed Christmas puddings of all time – certainly it turned out very well, blazing dramatically in its bath of brandy when I took it in on Christmas Day.

It was the Christmas Day, mainly, which made the month so memorable; I've never had, before or since, such a thoroughly delightful, hardworking, satisfying, traditional Christmas. The house was laden with holly, ivy, balloons, streamers stuck together drunkenly by eager little hands, mistletoe, bright paper Father Christmases cut out and painted laboriously by those children old enough to handle scissors and paint. Even the dogs had tinsel bows on their collars, which they were very good and patient about; less so the cats, who objected strongly and inflicted some very unfestive scratches on Caroline when she tried to decorate them in a suitable fashion. In the entrance hall stood the tall Christmas tree, brought in from somewhere on the farm – and for the first and only time in my life I saw a tree decorated with real candles, as well as angel-hair, baubles, tiny presents, and occasionally bits of chewed rusk and breadcrusts where the baby had contributed her bit to the family effort. On Christmas Eve it took ages, plus all the persuasive powers of the adults, to get the children off to bed; they were wildly excited, and even the baby got a bit beyond herself, catching the mood from the others. They were allowed to bring the presents they had made and wrapped themselves, and put them underneath the tree; so the untidy parcels were smuggled down underneath dressing-gowns and, in a great spirit of secrecy and among many hisses of 'Don't look! You mustn't look!' piled in a tumbled heap. I was surprised, and delighted, to see that there were some addressed to me, too.

At long last the children were all upstairs and if not in bed at least out of the way, although we heard the odd scuffle, giggle and pattering of footsteps until well after their usual bedtime. I sat at the kitchen table and started planning my campaign for the following day. The turkey was ready for the oven, only awaiting the rude intrusion of its stuffing first thing in the morning. The cake was ready and waiting. I hadn't had to make it, thank goodness, one of the grandparents had brought it – all I'd had to do was ice it, in the one and only style I know, the good old simple rough-snow effect. In this I'd been helped by the children, so there were one or two messy bits and a few dirty patches over which I had attached extra holly leaves and a rather unprepossessing robin. The pudding was ready for its final steaming. The cake tins bulged with mincepies. The brandy sauce and hard sauce were made. There only remained the vegetables to prepare. I decided it would work best to do these immediately, and leave them in cold water until the morning – blow the vitamin content for once, I didn't fancy peeling spuds and trimming sprouts for an hour or so first thing on Christmas morning. I was just about to heave the vast bag of sprouts on to the table and begin the marathon when Rodney arrived at the kitchen door. He had come to invite me in for a Christmas Eve drink, and it took all of half a second for me to decide that the sprouts could, after all, wait for the morning. So instead of spending my evening alone with the veg, I found myself part of a very merry gathering, sitting round the fire making considerable inroads into not only the sherry but the gin as well; it must have been one o'clock before we all retired to bed, not by any means as drunk as skunks but certainly happily relaxed and in festive mood.

On waking at six-thirty next morning, of course, things didn't look quite so jolly but by the time I'd showered and got to the kitchen I felt fine. I sneaked into the hall and placed the small presents I'd got for the children under the tree. The children themselves weren't long behind me, and I could hear their shrieks of excitement as I threw together a swift breakfast. The main presents, under the tree, were not to be opened until after lunch, but from the sound of it at least some of the parcels had been snitched from the pile. As soon as breakfast was over, to my great relief the two grandmothers and the niece arrived in the kitchen and, seating themselves round the table, got to work on the vegetables while I did indecent things to the turkey, bunged him in the oven and generally got on with the myriad things that always seem to have to be done at the last minute.

The meal went off perfectly – absolutely nothing went wrong, probably because it wouldn't have mattered if it had. The turkey was succulent, the roast spuds golden and crisp, and I didn't drop anything on the floor or into the sink; the pudding blazed, and the teenage niece found the wedding ring in her portion of it. Even Fred's having to leave the table precipitately due to a surfeit of cream couldn't spoil the mood. Diana, out of bed and feeling much better, helped the baby pull crackers but had to take the bang out first for her. I ate with them, at their insistence, leaping up and dashing out to the kitchen in relay with various relatives to fetch more mincepies, or cheese, or another pot of coffee or another bottle of wine, and by the time present-opening arrived we were all full of food, drink and sweet content. We sat in a big circle round the tree, and each person opened a present in turn. Mine from Fred was his second-favourite Dinky car, lovingly wrapped in pink loo paper; Caroline had made me a table mat, woven and fringed by herself; Maggie gave me a picture of her pony, drawn in crayon (I almost made the unforgivable mistake of thinking it was a dog); James had painted my portrait, a big circle for my head and body in one and two meandering lines for my legs; and the baby, with a little help from her friends, a piece of paper covered in kisses, all in different colours. They were all lovely presents. All the adu' present too, and I felt guilty that I hadn't reciprocated, but only for a moment; they were so warm and pleasant that I don't think it had ever occurred to them that I should. I received bottles of port and sherry (someone was a shrewd judge of character), a headscarf with horses on it (from one grandmother), string gloves with leather backs (the other grandmother), and from Rodney and Diana a very large and glossy cookery book.

Then the games began – but before that, the great moment of the Lighting of the Christmas Tree Candles. The teenage nephew Robert, and Rodney, rushed out into the yard and returned each with a long rod, at the top of which was fixed a sponge; they soaked the sponges in water, took up their positions one on each side of the tree, and all was in readiness for the ceremony. Diana, standing on a chair, lit a taper and very carefully set the flame to each candle. The lights were turned out, and the tree stood there in all its flickering glory, the flames reflecting on the baubles and spangles and tinsel, and the silver star on the very top. The children's faces were beautiful to see, and for once they were quiet, after the first indrawn breath of wonder. The baby said, 'Pretty', and stretched out her fat arms towards the tree, and then all the children were chattering and oohing and laughing, and it was time to get on with the games. The two sponge-bearers stayed near the tree, in case any of the flames got too ambitious; but none of them did. We played all the silly childhood games that get forgotten once you're grown-up, more's the pity; blind man's buff and grandmother's footsteps, statues and The Big Ship Sails Down the Alley-Alley-O. And then, as one of the grandmothers revealed an unsuspected gift for the piano, we played musical chairs and musical bumps and then, when the children were exhausted and had fallen on to the floor in heaps to rest, the adults danced Sir Roger de Coverley, up and down the hall, over and over again, as grandmother pounded the keys – occasionally the wrong ones – until we too were too tired to do any more dancing.

Now the candles were put out, and we all retired to the drawing room for tea and cake and more mincepies, having danced the last lot right away. After this it was time for a little sherry, and a small supper of cold turkey, and salad, and then time for tucking the exhausted children into their respective cots and beds. Just then, as we sat down round the fire for a final onslaught on the nuts and ～ ～e was a ring at the front door. I went to open it and there were the carol singers; real ones, who sang the carols all the way through by the light of a lantern, not a torch. They all had to be asked in, of course, and more mince pies heated and served, and a hot toddy made and drunk.

When I finally got to my bed, exhausted but exhilarated by the whole lovely day, the washing-up forgotten until the morning, I drew the curtain back and looked out over the paddocks. Such was the mood of the day, I expected to see snow falling and settling like feathers on the ground. Instead, there was a frost, and it was bright moonlight. Everywhere sparkled and glittered, like on those Christmas cards they used to have when I was a child. I stood and just looked at it all for a minute or two, and then let the curtain drop and, very happy indeed, fell into bed and straight to sleep.

Epilogue

The month at Barrow Farm turned out to be one of the last, as well as one of my pleasantest, housekeeping jobs. I was beginning to have strong urges for a place of my own, a front door I could close on the world, a more adequate income and the right to call my soul my own outside normal working hours. I had thoroughly enjoyed the last few years but enough was enough. I didn't want to end my days as a Faithful Old Retainer so, with a certain amount of regret, and some relief, I rejoined the ranks of those who earn their crust not by baking it but by raising dough in other ways.

It was back to the secretarial world where an untyped letter, unlike an unmade pudding, could always be dealt with the next morning. It was a more secure life out in the cold commercial world and a more remunerative one, but duller too and I was glad still to be studying for my degree – at least that was exciting and opened up a wider and a very different world. It introduced me to Art, Literature, Drama and a whole range of other interests. And, best of all, it introduced me to Himself.

'Come live with me and be my love,' said he. 'In Belfast.' So I did. And now I'm a housekeeper again. But with what a difference. Like all newly togethers we found out all sorts of things about each other which came as complete surprises. I found out he hated parsnips and kept seventeen shoes under his bed, each one clad cosily in a little protective fur coat of grey dust. He discovered that I was appallingly cheerful in the mornings and that his sitting-room carpet was green, something he had forgotten in the long years since he had actually seen it in the pile, as it were. He had no vacuum cleaner, and in an excess of zeal I went down on my hands and knees ⸻ whole place out with dustpan and brush. The resultant piles of fluff would have done credit to any old-time Western, rolling down the main drag of the deserted gold-strike town, driven before the desert winds. His myriad books were apparently chained to the wall, after the manner of the older university libraries; except that in his case the chains were spiders' webs of such tenacity that I had trouble wrenching his copy of *Twenty Years After* from their grasp. Naturally this exhibition of housewifely fervour didn't last very long; thankfully I found gainful outside employment very quickly and was able to go back to my usual practice of what the eye don't see the heart don't grieve over. Himself doesn't care whether I can even boil an egg, let alone whether it is done for precisely three and a half minutes; he wouldn't know what a cassoulet was if it got up and hit him, and he is very fond of beans on toast. He is also long accustomed to washing his own socks – and who am I to ask him to change the habits of a lifetime? Not only that, but he makes the best fry-up in the history of the universe; give him bacon, eggs, tomatoes, cold spuds, mushrooms, bread and about a pound of best butter and he can turn out an ambrosial meal fit for the gods. He also thinks I am the cat's whiskers, the bees' knees and the best thing since sliced bread. So you can understand why I don't mind throwing together the occasional meal and washing the odd shirt for him; the man may need his head examining, but he's one in a million!

Once we were Properly Married, we decided to go the whole hog and become bourgeois capitalist bloated plutocratic property owners; and in only another six years of crippling mortgage repayments we shall be the proud owners of our very own bijou fin-de-siècle converted artisan's cottage, with all mod cons and yet retaining certain charming period features. Or, in other words, a late Victorian terraced two-up and two-down with an indoor loo, lumpy plasterwork and a ghost on the stairs. We have as our constant companion and judgement upon us a direct descendant, or perhaps even a rein-carnation, of Cat; a small, parti-coloured, totally self-centred and innately baleful feline who answers, when she feels like it, to the name of Florence. Thanks to Florence, the entire house is not so much papered or decorated as upholstered in shag-pile; the multiple layers of woodchip paper with which the previous owners sought to cover a multitude of sins now hang in shreds on every wall from a height of about five feet and, in the places where she made an extra effort, up to six feet. As a result of these depredations by Florence, the house appears to be suffering from terminal dandruff.

Florence also preys mercilessly on the houseplants, of which we had, at last count, fifty-seven, which isn't bad going for a house without windowsills, porch or backyard. Fighting your way into the bathroom is like penetrating the upper reaches of the Orinoco, while the kitchen needs only a parrot or two to add the finishing touch. Sometimes, struggling to cram just one more plant pot on to the end of the bath, or wandering aimlessly round the house seeking space for yet another thriving geranium cutting, I recall the spacious acres of Crumbling Court and wonder what it looks like now. I don't ever want to go back and see, in case it is unbearable. Watching Florence beating up her toy rabbit, I think of The Mob and wonder what she would have made of them; hamburger, probably. (We are convinced that her father was either a globe-trotting Tasmanian devil or a peripatetic sabre-tooth tiger.) As I drape Himself's shirts over the radiators prior to flinging them, unpressed, on to a hanger, I remember the handiwork of Cyril, that master of the steam-iron, with the piles of snowy pristine shirts rising like miniature Matterhorns around his ironing board. I cook our economical meals and contrast their frugality with the lavishness of the Middle Easterners' diet; I put away our two plates and Florence's saucer and recall the endless hours of drudgery over strange sinks for even stranger employers; I think of all those poor unfortunates for whom I worked, and of those who deserved no better than they got. And I particularly think of those I wish I could see again, and know I never shall.

And then I look round our tiny living room, where only a generation ago families as large as Diana's brood were brought up by mothers with no washing machines, no tumble-driers, no gadgets at all – indeed, without electricity; and I wonder how the devil they managed it. I look at the books – slightly less cobwebby now, but not much – the pictures, the detritus of hobbies in progress, the dust-attracting collection of ornaments, each with its particular and very special relevance, the cluster of plants.

Everything I can see is appreciated, enjoyed and loved. I look at Florence, lost in the sheepskin rug in front of the fire, kneading the deep wool in a sensuous dream of World Domination as She Knows It, which means Himself and me. I look at Himself, sitting there in his armchair, not saying much, reading or watching the television or working on something, lighting his pipe ten times for every puff he gets out of it, and heavens, I feel happy.

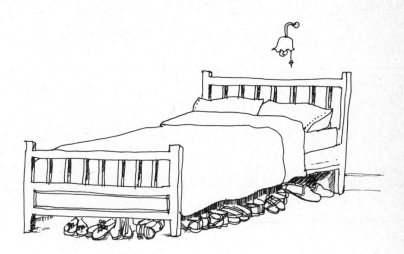